THIS
*Re*IMAGINED
EMPTY NEST

A Life, Repurposed Compilation

THIS
*Re*IMAGINED
EMPTY NEST

MICHELLE RAYBURN
AND FRIENDS

FAITH CREATIVITY
LIFE BOOKS

"My thoughts are nothing like your thoughts,"
says the LORD. "And my ways are far beyond
anything you could imagine."

Isaiah 55:8

Contents

Embracing Change and Self-Discovery

Finding Passion and Purpose

Celebrating Relationships and Connections

Introduction

MICHELLE RAYBURN

AS YOUR CHILDREN LEAVE HOME, perhaps you find yourself at a cross-roads with mixed emotions: pride, nostalgia, celebration, sadness, and possibly some apprehension. Your once-bursting-with-energy home now feels quieter. The sounds of play, television shows, band practice, and laughter once filled the silence, but now you hear the ticking of the wall clock. Perhaps you're excited and eager for a chapter that's been on your mind for a while. What now?

This book is a companion for you. The twenty-two writers who contributed their heartfelt thoughts and wisdom have been there too. We want you to know that while we've seen the challenges that come with this period, we have also discovered opportunities to grow, rediscover, and experience newfound freedom.

We'll cover embracing change and self-discovery, finding passion and purpose, and celebrating relationships and connections. And we'll offer gentle reminders that in this tender time, nurturing your own well-being and deepening connections with your spouse are important as you redefine your identity beyond the role of a mom. We hope you'll laugh too.

This metaphor of an "empty nest" has been around for at least a century and isn't going anywhere. But it's a terrible picture when you pick the analogy apart. A bird empties the nest and then fills it again, some having multiple sets of baby birds in a season. I have no intention of giving birth again. None. Besides, have you ever seen a mother bird just sitting on an empty nest chilling out there? And have you ever seen a nest with ten birds all crammed in for a family reunion? I dislike the image of chicks leaving and never returning!

So we will use this metaphor, imagining a quaint picture of sweet bird mamas sitting on our feathered bowls made of twigs and straw while our fledglings find their way in the world, and we shall leave science out of it altogether. Otherwise, it will wreck us.

Although these are our stories, this book is a mirror reflecting your resilience and strength too. I hope you'll see your story in ours. Some of us did fully choreographed dances when our children left home, and others curled up in bed and sobbed. There is no right way to get through this transition outside of leaning on each other. Our stories are still unfolding too. Perhaps you're are raising fledgling grandchildren after having some years of quiet. Or you stepped into foster care or adoption without expecting it. Your nest might be difficult to define.

Reimagining is the process of recreating or forming a new conception of your future. While the nest might be empty, *you* are *full* of endless possibilities—maybe ones that are different from what you envisioned and even with unwanted heartaches thrown in there. This is a time for self-discovery, for finding new passions and purposes. Hope takes us beyond what we can see and keeps us pressing forward, and we're so glad you joined us on the journey from nest to next.

Embracing Change and Self-Discovery

Release

BETH BARRON

I write this poem to you, my youngest son,
whom I clasped in my arms, and my admonitions,
whose exuberance thrust me aside.
Slim and slight and fleet,
you escaped to the creek with your tribe,
canon-balled down from a frayed rope
to explode the waters below,
celebrating your independence with battle whoops.

You created the Order of Adolescence,
marked your membership with dirt war paint.
I kept watch for you to return home
to abandon your dripping cut-offs to mildew.
I labored to shape and contain you,
but you embraced brownstones, Arabic,
and classmates with flawless resumes.

I feared your choices, while you reveled in your options:
lentils with cumin in Cairo, stifling heat in Oman.
Now, your tribe dons tasteful ties with suits or pea coats
and shapes the world with corporate mergers.

Escaping your Fifth Avenue office for lunch,
you startle me with your deepened voice on the phone.
Christmas draws you home to clasp me in an awkward hug
and to breakdance in the snow with your brothers.

I open my arms
and write this poem to release you to your tribe,
my son.

Fly, Mama, Fly

MICHELLE RAYBURN

NURTURING AND CARING FOR CHILDREN until they leave home can be a depleting process. There. I said it. It's beautiful to bring them from helpless fledglings to full-grown fliers. But this is hard stuff. If your bank account has ever been on its last fumes, running on vapors like a car chugging along and hoping for a downhill slope, you know what I mean. Baseball shoes and pizza. Laptops, gadgets, and gaming consoles. And pizza. Music lessons, medical bills, travel, uniforms, school supplies. And pizza. College, cars, light bills, and prom.

That's just the bank account. How is your energy? You've been on an emotional rollercoaster with teens in the recent past. Social drama. Enough said.

Are you OK? Can I bring a casserole or bath salts? Maybe a latte? Or a punching bag? I hope you're starting to catch up on the last twenty-five years of lost sleep. Yes, I'm aware that worry about your adult child has a lost-sleep factor of its own. I've texted a college-aged son to ask, "Are you alive? I saw a news story about a kayaker lost in the river, and they're looking for his identity. You have a kayak…"

He tortured us on that one with the delay of his response. It probably wasn't even intentional. He once lost his phone in a snowbank for six months, but I had texted it in case someone found it. Meanwhile, he borrowed and activated my old flip phone. With the spring thaw came a strange call that led to stopping our minivan at the curb of an apartment in a sketchy part of town, where he retrieved said phone from a very nice but very scary-looking dude who had found it in the post-winter gunk and charged it up. You are correct to insist that young adult children are not worry-free.

Overall, though, the empty nest is a chance for you to get a little of your old color back.

> The empty nest is a chance for you to get a little of your old color back.

Birds of a Feather

I recently learned something about flamingos and their color. At first, it actually sounded like an urban legend, so I did a little investigating. And it turns out the San Diego Zoo had something to say about it, so it wasn't fabricated but science. Flamingos create a nest from a mound of mud. Nothing fancy. That really sums up how I raised my boys. Mud. Nothing fancy or breakable. But wait. There's more.

The flamingo lays one chalky white egg that hatches in the mud nest. Until the little chick can eat on its own, the parents feed it "crop milk." This is not a discussion to have at the dinner table, but this "milk" comes from somewhere in a parent bird's digestive tract and is regurgitated to the little baby bird. This process temporarily changes the parents' plumage to the point where they turn white or pale pink instead of the bright pinkish hue we're familiar with.[1] There's a bunch of science behind this, but essentially, the flamingo gets its color from what it eats. And feeding a chick depletes them of their own energy and nutrients. When the chick becomes independent, the parent begins to get its color back.

The thing is, this is a natural part of raising the chick. And it doesn't permanently hurt the flamingo. It's just different. When that little one can fish for its own food, it turns pink too.

Flocking Together

Mom, you're starting to get your color back. You've been known for years as so-and-so's mom. Perhaps being a mom has been where you've invested your time and energy and money for a few decades because the kids have been the center of your world. But you have a first name. You know how to manage a home and a job, have picked up amazing skills, and are a bundle of creative energy waiting for a new outlet. And when you start to turn pink again, your children do too. They flourish and thrive when they see you in full color.

> Mom, you're starting to get your color back. You've been known for years as so-and-so's mom.

Here are a few ways I've found my pink:

Spending quality time with my husband. We have a much more playful way of communicating with one another, and we're intentional about spending designated time together. We also validate our individual interests and encourage each other to pursue and enjoy those hobbies.

Heartfelt conversations with our kids. One of the best parts of having adult children is the deep conversations we sometimes have about life stuff. We can even disagree on things and respect each other. From theology to books to movies and entertainment, it's fun to cultivate conversations that feel more like friendships, replacing orders to clean their rooms and do their chores with more entertaining topics. I've even heard words of gratitude that melt my heart as they reflect on our parenting them over the years.

Organizing and decorating. I've spent a few years purging closets and cupboards and doing some redecorating. The house stays cleaner and more organized, which brings a sense of peace to my daily routine. The decorating, repainting, and remodeling bring out my creative side. Developing a new career in this half of life has helped fund the renovations.

Self-care. I love spending an afternoon reading in the hammock. Or relaxing on a Sunday afternoon with a feel-good movie. It can look like pampering, but more often it looks like advocating for my need for some quiet space.

Serving others. After the children were in college, I took on more roles at church—different ones from the areas where I served when they were involved. I also recently ran for school board and now serve my community in that role. It's satisfying to be part of something that is greater than myself and outside the walls of our home.

Pursuing meaningful work. I went into the workforce after taking a break to raise children. It helped me rediscover my old passions and uncover new ones. I love the creative work I do, and it provides a sense of accomplishment and satisfaction.

Finding Your Wings

We're all wired differently. For some, your color will come back when you connect with old and new friends. It might be in artistic expression or travel. Some empty nesters will become daycare providers for grandchildren—God bless you. We each find our own balance between caring for and serving others and loving ourselves and tending to our needs.

You can be selective with your time and your money. Your wardrobe and hair and makeup might change. Your bedtime might be earlier or later now. The grocery bill will diminish, and you'll make fewer trips to the store. It's surprising how one child's departure might cut the laundry loads in half—all that clean stuff they keep re-washing from the floor makes a difference. You won't need to hide your favorite cookies in the crisper.

> Now that your nest is empty, it's time to spread those wings.

Perhaps the metaphor of the empty nest has been over-applied to the chicks leaving and fluttering away. Mom, you have wings too.

Now that your nest is empty, it's time to spread those wings. You've spent years nurturing and caring for your children—raised amazing kids! It's time to explore new interests, survey the horizon for new challenges, and seize opportunities with confidence. Your pink is coming back.

Fly, mama, fly!

The Color of the Carolina Wren

MAUREEN MILLER

SHE LANDED ON A BRIGHT, late-March morning, suitcase in hand.
My husband, Bill, and I thought we would soon to be empty nesters, at least in the coming three or four years. But with Allie's arrival, all that changed, and in the blink of her brown eyes.

We adopted our sons at birth, and they were teenagers by the spring of 2012. Though it would still be some time before my husband and I found ourselves without children in the home, we'd begun to dream. What trips would we take? What meals would we make?

It's not that we were looking forward to this new season. Not at all. We just knew it was coming. Furthermore, the notion we'd have a daughter was furthest from our minds. After all, we'd already lost two through failed adoptions, and I knew I was made to be a mother of boys.

Loss so Deep

When we received the phone call only a week earlier from my friend Cindy—the woman who's also our oldest son's birth mom, who, after her personal experience, chose to work in the adoption field—my heart picked up pace.

"A little girl in South Carolina . . . needing a forever family . . . suffered loss . . . immediate placement . . . thought of you."

Was it meant to be us? Were we the ones? Should we say yes?

> Was it meant to be us? Were we the ones? Should we say yes?

Not quite three years old nor fully potty-trained, Allie had already been adopted once. Her maternal grandfather became her adoptive father with the strike of a gavel earlier that year. Two months later, while she ate Cheerios in her highchair, Papa Jimmy, as she affectionately called him, suffered a massive heart attack, passing away only hours later.

We talked to our boys. "What do you think about adding a little sister?"

They were in. Excited, in fact. After all, we'd each grieved the other losses, especially the more recent one in 2007. The little girl we'd hoped to add to our family was the same age as our son Jake, only a year and a half younger than our oldest son, Ian, but after a year, she was gone.

This was another opportunity to have a sister, someone they could teach to swim and fish, to snuggle with on the couch, to protect as only big brothers could.

On that early spring Saturday, Allie arrived with her uncle and "Bunny"—a grandmother figure who'd been Papa Jimmy's longtime girlfriend. We'd invited them to come visit our North Carolina farm, meet our dogs, not to mention several extended family members. "See if you think we could be her forever home," we'd added, knowing these people who loved this little girl were, like her, also grieving the death of a man they loved. Could they part with her, especially after so much recent loss?

Questions so Great

It happened to be Palm Sunday weekend. The plan was for Allie's uncle to leave her and Bunny with us, given all seemed good and safe. He'd return on Monday to retrieve them. Then, back home in South Carolina, they'd determine the next step.

So, when the discussion quickly turned that Saturday afternoon to signing temporary guardianship papers, my heart thumped in my chest. Was this really happening? Was it too soon?

Memories of our first attempt to add a daughter flooded my mind, and I recalled how quickly everything happened. How we felt so sure. How, even at the hospital on the day of her birth, everyone seemed on board. But then how, just after our first night together, the lawyer came and whisked her away, stating, "Her birth mom couldn't go through with it. She's changed her mind." All I knew was I never got to say goodbye.

> The questions swirled. Even more, however, was a peace that surpassed all understanding.

And it could happen again. Was my heart prepared for that torment? What if Allie's uncle left, then returned on Monday as planned, only to get home and realize it was simply too hard to let her go?

But there were other questions as well. After years of being a family of four, me being a mother of boys, how would adding a fifth—this time, a daughter—change the dynamic? Would Allie come with brokenness we'd not know how to fix? Were we the right family for her?

The questions swirled. Even more, however, was a peace that surpassed all understanding—something we couldn't quite explain. And before Allie's uncle left, we signed the documents he'd prepared. Then, after a day visiting and getting to know one another over good food and perfect weather, we said goodbye to the man Allie called "Un-tle S-tott."

Love so Tender

God has a sweet sense of humor, always knowing exactly what his children need, adding confirmation, affirmation, and a glimmer of his will when we're not quite sure. Though this toddler—the little one who'd experienced more loss than some do in a lifetime—was not yet three, she'd bring his message. And to this mother's ears, hers was a melody lovelier than the song sparrow's.

> God has a sweet sense of humor, always knowing exactly what his children need.

I'd offered to give Allie a bath before bedtime, her Bunny already cozy in our guest room, tucked in with a good book. In a tub filled with warm sudsy water, Allie played with bath toys, splashing and singing quietly to herself, many of the songs ones I'd not heard in some time. Despite having just met me, she was comfortable and content—winsome, in a two-year-old sort of way.

Prior to toweling her off, we reviewed who she'd met that day. I'd say a name, and Allie would repeat after me.

"Aunt Katie."

"Aunt Ta-tie."

"Uncle Garret."

"Un-tle D-arret."

"Nana."

"Nana."

"Cousin Ali Beth."

"T-ousin A-wi Be-ff."

"Bill."

"Bill."

"Ian."

"I-wan."

"Jacob."

"D-acob."

Finally, I pointed to myself. "And who am I?"

Initially, I'd introduced myself with my nickname, knowing it would be easier for a toddler to pronounce. But before I could say *Mo*, then have her repeat, the little girl with eyes the color of the Carolina wren paused a moment, then smiled.

"Momma."

Time so Precious

And right then, I knew. Bill's and my plans for an empty nest could wait another sixteen years. Maybe more. Because a little one named Allie was meant to find a dwelling with us—that spot without a daughter no longer vacant but perfectly filled with the girl God intended.

Later, I heard God's whisper as I read the psalmist's words: "Even the sparrow finds a home, and the swallow builds her nest and raises her young" (Psalm 84:3).

Indeed, a little bird had joined our nest, her presence making our family complete. She'd not expected to land in a place apart from those familiar, all whom she loved. But God, in his kindness, had a plan, using a toddler to tell us.

And as always, God's plan is perfect.

Hitting Your Stride

LINDA HANSTRA

I T'S BEEN SIX YEARS SINCE my husband and I transitioned to our empty nest. I recall looking forward to all the free time I would finally have. I was also terrified of all the free time I would finally have.[2]

Would I be able to fill that time with anything worthwhile? Would my life still have meaning without the flurry of activities that surrounded the kids? I fretted that my life, like our nest, would feel empty.

Perhaps your youngest (or only) child has just moved out of the house, and your nest is empty. How's it going? Do you cry every time you walk past their empty room? Or are you jumping for joy at your newfound freedom?

Having mixed emotions is normal. So is a time of adjustment.

Looking back, I can see that the adjustment to an empty nest happened in three stages. For me, each one was a necessary part of the process. The first two stages were a matter of survival, while the third one helped me thrive.

Before I explain these three stages, let me digress with a little biking backdrop.

The Straight Trail

Once our nest was empty, we filled much of our newfound free time with biking. It filled up our spare hours and was good for our health and our spirits. (In fact, when we've taken part in organized rides, we've noticed most bikers are empty nesters and retirees. Now we fit right in!)

We spend time in Minnesota every summer, where there are several lakeside and wooded bike trails we love. Each trail offers something different and its own unique experience.

As we ride around Lake Bemidji, the four-mile stretch through the state park is as straight as an arrow. It follows an old rail bed and provides occasional lovely lake views. I enjoy the peacefulness and predictability of this long, straight path.

But to be honest, the long, straight paths can get boring. There aren't many surprises since you can see what's ahead for miles. The monotony makes the trail seem longer than it is in reality.

The Curvy Trail

By contrast, the most exciting trails are the curvy ones that wind their way through the woods. My favorite, the Migizi Trail, bends and twists through pine and birch forests. Not knowing what's around the next curve adds to the thrill of the ride. Will I find something wild and wonderful that will take my breath away? Like a deer. A fox. A patch of wildflowers. Or a stunning sunset over the lake.

> The most exciting trails are the curvy ones that wind their way through the woods.

Or might danger be lurking around the bend? Like another rider on the wrong side of the path. Water across the trail. A skunk. A bear. Or a fallen tree.

One frequent surprise on our Minnesota trail rides is turtles. When I stop to take a picture, they usually scurry away. One time, I came across an overly fearful one. She pulled her head, legs, and tail into her shell and didn't move. Frozen with fear and unwilling to face the scary person with the iPhone camera, she just sat there.

CHOOSING A PATH

The trails and turtles are a perfect illustration of the three steps I took in transitioning to my empty nest. Perhaps you also went through these steps as well or are going through them now.

Which stage we enter and how long we linger there depends on our own needs, situation, hopes, and dreams. We each choose our own path.

First, We Might Hide

When my last baby left home, I admit I crawled into my shell for a couple of weeks. I cried for no apparent reason. I lacked the motivation to do anything more than necessary. I didn't want to go anywhere. Like that overwhelmed turtle, I couldn't move.

> There's no right or wrong amount of time to grieve our losses.

Each of us handles the emotions of loss, fear, and uncertainty on our own terms. There's no right or wrong amount of time to grieve our losses. If hiding in your shell is right for you for a time, then that is what you should do.

But if you feel yourself becoming smaller and the shell becoming bigger, it might be time to seek help or call a friend. There are many books and online resources that specifically address the challenges of empty nesting. Seeking help can be the first step to moving on in your journey.

Next, We Get Out And Ride

Riding a straight path is an improvement over turtle-in-the-shell mode. At least we're moving forward. We're finding our ruts and staying the course. There is comfort in routine, and there is nothing wrong with that. Routines create a sense of order. When our lives turn upside down overnight by the departure of our last child, keeping a sense of order is a necessary part of survival.

For me, "riding the straight path" was working at my job, tending my gardens, going to church, and cleaning my house. It included Netflix, books, and music. Whatever feels comfortable and routine to you, whether it's work or play, keep doing it! Stay the course and move along. Riding the straight path is peaceful and predictable.

As in biking, this path can also be monotonous, offering little in the way of potential and possibility. The excitement and surprises our kids brought to our lives are missing, leaving us in a midlife rut. It might be time to aim for step three of the empty-nest transition.

Finally, We Hit Our Stride

If you truly want meaning and purpose during the empty nest years, then it's time to branch out and chase your dreams. Like the curvy bike trail with surprises around every bend, maybe something wonderful awaits you! What new hobby, side hustle, career, or adventure did you put on hold while you were busy raising your kids? Now is your time!

After spending a year in our predictable life patterns, I put on my "Brave" helmet and took a chance on myself. I had dabbled in writing before, but signing up for an online writing class was a big step outside my comfort zone. I was filled with doubts and fears, but taking that challenge has provided me with more rewards than I ever imagined.

As a couple, we also saw new possibilities in our empty nest. We explored new cities, landscapes, and other attractions by car, bike, boat, and on foot. We tackled our bucket list of dreams, checking off goals along the way.

> It's time to branch out and chase your dreams.

Possibilities continued to present themselves. We prayed for guidance and protection as we rounded each bend in the road and prepared to stop and re-route if we hit a roadblock. We often reached out to friends to help us overcome life's hurdles.

Along that curvy path, we found unexpected events—some difficult, others joyous. I cared for and said goodbye to my parents. We became grandparents two times over. We struggled through a pandemic. We found our cabin up north. I retired from my day job and published my first book.

Hitting our stride on this curvy, bendy trail of life brings hills and valleys, thrills and chills. But taking it all in—the quiet and smooth, the rough and risky—is all part of the ride. The empty-nest joyride!

Dear Mom, You're Getting Schooled

RUTHIE GRAY

D ID YOU JUST DROP YOUR firstborn child off at college? Are you bawling your eyes out, wondering if life will ever be the same again? I feel you, mama.

The first child out the door signals the beginning of a new era. I remember dropping my oldest off in her first year of college. It's a big step for moms, like the first day of kindergarten. If you have a few other children still tucked in the nest, it softens the blow somewhat, yet the feeling looms that life as you know it will never be the same again.

(You would be correct in that assumption, by the way.)

I once saw a video of a mom hanging off the back of a car as her daughter drove joyfully off to college. If you feel like that right now, I've got news for you.

It gets worse.

Learning the Drill

At one point, we had *three of our four* children institutionalized at the same time. (The parents weren't far from it, either.)

Four kids. *Eleven* college years. Thirty-seven semesters. Five campuses. Four states. Three girls. One boy.

No partridges.

Their father and I dripped mental sweat out of our pores as if we had just run a marathon. Prepare to be put through the wringer. What's more (I hate to tell you), your kid is not the one getting schooled. You are.

> Your kid is not the one getting schooled. You are.

The following events may or may not have happened throughout our children's college tenure. (Who am I kidding—they all happened. I can't make this stuff up, although I wish I could say I had.)

While attending college, your child may change majors six to ten times. When happily skipping out of the nest, they might not care what major they choose, so long as they're out from under Mom and Dad's rule. "It'll all work out," they reason as they dart from social event to sorority signing, thereby focusing on the truly important things in their educational life.

Finance Exercises

There are things called "meal tickets," which often take a backseat to more glamorous options when one has a kitchen right in their dorm quad. Running up your (the parents') credit card on "groceries" seems perfectly logical to the college student.

Since groceries can be justified as a logical expense, the student may opt to spend the day shopping instead of attending class (again, your credit card). You will not discover this bit of information until American Express delivers your monthly statement.

You also won't know she skipped class because the time of purchase isn't logged on said statement. (You will find out later, when she brings a friend home who accidentally mentions the shopping trip took place during social economics class.)

While cultivating her social talents, your child will sometimes feel it necessary to treat friends, Romans, and countrymen—aka acquaintances—to dinner at the Olive Garden not just once, but multiple times (again, courtesy of your credit card and no thanks to the meal ticket).

Communication Tests

They opt out of texting or calling for weeks. ("Mom, I'm sooooo busy!" Read: "I can't talk right now. There's a party in my dorm. Actually, it's in my room. Brb. Jk.")

For reference: Brb = Be right back. Jk = Just kidding. The acronym vocabulary drastically increased since our kids were students. Might wanna brush up on that. Put IMO (in my opinion) in your back pocket for a few minutes from now.

Sons bring a whole different vibe to the college scene. Your son could potentially participate in a "compost pile," which would be great if it was an approved, organized activity for the benefit of all involved.

However, when it includes hoarding and tossing cafeteria fruit out the dorm window and onto the front lawn, it could be construed as damaging college property. Especially when a collection of oranges, mango slices, and banana peelings ends up on cars in the adjacent lot or a melon shatters a windshield.

Since children are, well, still children when they leave at the age of eighteen (IMO), and they've chosen to leave for the first available college to get out from under your thumb, they might later regret their institutional choice. This results in a switching of educational facilities. In our case, it happened three more times.

Did you know it's possible to attend school so long that you accidentally graduate from a college you previously attended? It is, indeed.

After blowing through three colleges, the former dean called over Christmas break to say, "Well, you're graduated! Congratulations!"

(Mom and dad breathed a collective sigh of relief.)

Professional student, anyone?

Pivot and Patience Practice

When your young adult (we'll humor them with this title) decides college is not for them after attending a semester, they may announce their desire to pursue a cheaper option—such as beauty school—while commuting from home. In our case, this young adult proceeded to drop out of the first college without ever attending beauty school and, instead, produced a bachelor of arts after blowing through two more institutions. ("I never really liked that first school, Mom.")

Some colleges are close to home, and some are not. We enjoyed the pleasure of both, with the closest being ten minutes down the road. Consequently, on more than one nightly occasion, we returned home only to find our family room dark and full of young men with weird hair watching even weirder movies and eating our food.

(When this happens, roll with it because boys are fun, drama-free refrigerator raiders. Your sides will split with laughter, enabling you to cope with the grocery bills.)

Unplanned visits also occur from college campuses located miles away, complete with carloads of girls and surprise speeding tickets.

Your directionally challenged child may even send a quick text, "Headed home, see you in three hours!" only to call two hours later to inform you of an accidental turn, resulting in a re-route back to campus. "See you in three more hours . . ." (You are still paying for all that gas.)

Campus apartments can be scary, even when carefully selecting the cleanest, most affordable studio apartment you can find via online advertisements from miles away. Despite your best efforts, you may not be prepared for the actual up-close, in-person version of said apartment.

You may even burst into tears.

And that same kid might possibly phone home to announce a crime scene of which they were an accidental victim, complete with a bullet hole in their apartment window. ("Hey, Mom, I just got interviewed by the police!")

Lecture-Free Learning

On the upside, you will be entertained on many occasions by your college child's antics. Like receiving a text photo of a bottle of mousse your kid accidentally toted around to class all morning instead of a water bottle.

> In the grand scheme of things, four years is not that long.

In the grand scheme of things, four years is not that long, but to a student, their college tenure seems like forever. Be prepared for your child to ask if quitting is an option every. single. day. ("Just checking, Dad!")

It wasn't.

Even so, your young adult may once again decide their college of choice is not delivering the goods or meeting their expectations. They may take on a "summer job" that extends fourteen months, thereby enjoying a welcome hiatus. ("The job lasted longer than I thought it would.")

After the hiatus, they may switch colleges to major in the choice *you* suggested in the first place because "my boss said I'd be good at it."

(I hope you can feel my eyes rolling right through the vellum.)

Your child will likely graduate (eventually) and get a job totally unrelated to her field. It's okay. Go with God. Be blessed. Thank the LORD she is done and the bills are not still mounting.

(You're just stuck with the aftermath. Jehovah Jireh: the Lord provides.)

Love Lessons

Lastly, and this will probably happen with at least one of your children, the college grad may move back home. But only for a season. And if you keep your heart right, it'll be one more sweet chance to savor their presence before they get out and leave you alone.

Fellow mom, here's the rule of life: nothing will happen the way you think it will.

> The rule of life: nothing will happen the way you think it will.

Prepare yourself and cease the stressing. Help them make decisions (if they'll let you), fill out the FAFSA, pay your part of the college bill, send the rest to Sallie Mae, and sit back and wait for the next surprise. It'll happen. I guarantee it.

But you will survive.

(And so will your kid.)

Threads of Letting Go

JENN DAFOE-TURNER

THE SALTINESS FROM MY TEARS reached the corners of my mouth as I cried, "God, I don't understand why my baby boy doesn't want to spend time with me." Even though I was grossly ignoring the fact that my eldest son was now in his twenties and married, my chest tightened, and my mind reeled with this startling realization.

I knew this eight-hour drive home would be good for me, giving me time to weep and mourn the loss that my mama's heart was feeling. Throughout my entire trip to see Sam, he wanted to do everything with everyone except me. The sting of his rejection was worse than a bee's, and it broke me.

The Fabric of Growing

I knew the umbilical cord was severed years ago, but the invisible thread connecting our hearts never faded. Every first milestone was shared—his first steps where he stumbled into my loving embrace, the first time he said "Mama" was music to my ears, and his first day of school when he clung to me, his tiny fingers entwined tightly with mine. Our bond was an all-encompassing, soulful dance of love and trust, a rhythm only known between a mother and her child.

Years of whispered bedtime stories, shared laughter over silly jokes, and comforting hugs during inevitable scrapes and bruises. While riding on the city bus, he looked up at me with his big, warm blackish/brown eyes and said, "Mommy, just call me Sweetie." These were the threads that intricately wove our mother-son tapestry. This was the little boy I still saw.

Today, though, as the sun was rising, trying to poke through the clouds to greet the day, I was driving my truck and having one of the biggest pity parties. I wanted my baby boy back. I wanted to be the number-one girl in his life. I wanted to be the only one to call him Sweetie.

> I still wanted him to need his mom. But he didn't.

Even though I loved his wife and the man he was, I still wanted him to need his mom. But he didn't. And today, I became brutally aware of this truth. Our three younger children still needed me, and if I couldn't handle one child not needing me anymore, what would happen when the other three followed suit?

Embroidered in Memories

As I navigated the winding roads, my mind took a similar path, unraveling memories of Sam at various stages of his life. The hum of the truck's engine was a low soundtrack to the vivid recollections playing in my mind. I saw a dark-eyed toddler, his gap-toothed grin shining brighter than any sun as he chased birds in our backyard. I could almost hear his infectious giggle as he popped a bubble he had just blown, his eyes reflecting the wonder of the world he was beginning to explore.

Then he metamorphosed into a lanky teenager, his face a battleground of adolescence, yet his spirit unbroken, full of dreams and promises. I remembered our late-night talks when he'd share his fears and aspirations, his voice barely above a whisper, as if even mentioning them aloud might shatter them.

Finally, I saw him transform into the man he is today. His face now bore the lines of maturity, but his eyes were the same, reflecting his heart full of love, kindness, and strength I was so proud of. Every memory and every image was a tender stitch in the fabric of our shared journey, a journey that was no longer just ours. As the miles passed under the tires of my truck, I found myself immersed in these memories, a silent observer of the passage of time and the growth of my baby boy into a man.

Hemmed in Gratitude

I don't know when the weather changed, but I was suddenly in the sun as I drove the winding highway intermingled with my trip down memory lane. As the clouds moved from my view to give clear skies, my thoughts began to do the same.

> The Lord began to use those memories to bring up a wellspring of gratitude for who my son was becoming.

The Lord began to use those memories to bring up a wellspring of gratitude for who my son was becoming. I saw the impact of my love, my prayers, and the lessons I had taught him reflected in his character, his choices, and his relationships. As I continued to release the pain of letting go, a new understanding took root: it's okay to let go and watch him soar.

In this world that values independence and self-reliance above all else, it can be challenging for a mother to let go of her child and accept they're no longer needed in the same way. But as I drove toward home, my heart aching but also overflowing with gratitude and love, God showed me that letting go doesn't mean losing him. It simply means acknowledging his growth and his own journey, one in which I was blessed to help shape, for good or bad.

Seeing him love his wife and, eventually, his son is beautiful. If I were still the number one woman in his life, I shudder to think of what my daughter-in-love and grandson would be missing out on. And it's beautiful to see them flourish—to see the fruits of our labor and love blossom into something beyond what we could ever imagine.

> I can let go and give my son his own wings to fly.

God opened my eyes to know and understand the memories I will always cherish, which are the threads that connect us. Because of this, I can let go and give my son his own wings to fly. In doing so, our bond has only strengthened, and we are now rooted in mutual love and respect for each other's individual paths. We both look forward to the times our paths intersect, whether over Sunday dinner or a family vacation.

Stitched by Love

God's transformation in me has completely changed our relationship, while nothing has changed. We still continue to treat one another the same. We laugh. We joke. We cry. We talk. We encourage. We pray. We are secure in our love for one another.

Letting go of our adult children is hard but worth the rich friendship that develops. It's okay to feel the pain during the process, while embracing the beauty of watching your child grow into their own person is worth it. This is another chapter in our ever-changing relationship with our children.

Much like the evolving relationship between parents and their grown children, our spiritual walk mirrors this transformational bond. Just as we mothers learn to adapt in our roles from caregivers to guides, continuing to root for our child from the sidelines, our heavenly Father adopts a similar stance in our faith journeys. He nurtures us in our early stages of faith, enveloping us in his unwavering support and love. Yet, as we grow, he encourages us to explore, question, and even struggle, knowing these experiences will deepen our trust in him.

The friendships we develop with God through every trial and triumph become testaments to his patience and enduring presence in our lives. He delights in our growth, cherishing the mature, reciprocal companionship that emerges as we deepen our belief and understanding. Through this divine dynamic, we come to realize our relationship with God, much like a parent's love, transcends mere dependency—it flourishes into a beautiful, ongoing dialogue of mutual respect and affection.

Woven on the Heart

In the quietude of these reflections, I've come to recognize the profound, interwoven tapestry of love, loss, growth, and rebirth that epitomizes the mother-child relationship. It's a divine cycle, echoing the eternal rhythm of seasons under heaven's gaze. In letting go, we find ourselves holding on to something far greater—unseen threads of unbreakable bonds woven by shared memories, lessons, and love. This dance of release and embrace teaches us the true essence of love's power: to free and to bind in the same breath.

> In letting go, we find ourselves holding on to something far greater.

I stand now, not just as a mother, but as a witness to the miraculous unfolding of life, guided by a faith that transforms, a love that liberates, and a hope that whispers renaissance in every goodbye.

In my son's flight, I've found my own wings. In letting go, I've embraced the vast expanse of love's true legacy, knowing it is part of God's design from the beginning. "A man leaves his father and mother and is joined to his wife, and the two are united into one" (Genesis 2:24).

Finding Joy in the Empty Nest

SHARON SUNKLE

T CAME FAST. ONE DAY I was changing diapers, wiping jelly off their faces, and holding their little hands while walking. The next day, I was saying goodbye to them at their college dorm.

A New Season

I said goodbye to our first son of three at his college and cried almost half the way home of a four-hour drive. But in the middle of the drive, I began to think about all the irritating things he had done over the summer after his graduation from high school. Irritations included coming in late from curfew, not cleaning up after himself, taking my wet clothes out of the washer and putting them on the floor so that he could wash his own clothes.

Remembering these incidents, I began to feel a little better, knowing I wouldn't have to deal with those irritations any longer. Sounds like I wanted to forget about him, doesn't it? Ha! No way. I was just relieved to not have to deal with these frustrations for the time being. And I still had two more boys at home who needed mothering.

Seeing the second son go off to college was a little easier but still hard and brought abundant tears. I didn't cry too long, however, knowing that this one was totally ready for the challenges of college life. At this point, I had gone back to college myself, received my degree, and was pursuing a career of my own. And I still had one more at home.

Taking the last son to college was especially sad and depressing, as I felt my parenting days were over. But I've found nothing could have been further from the truth. These boys didn't need me to be a hands-on mom any longer, but they still needed me, just in a different way. Mothering took on a different role.

> They still needed me, just in a different way.

They needed a friend, a confidant, an encourager, and a prayer warrior. This was the new definition of myself as a parent. I was excited for our third-born son to grow his wings. He was always ahead of himself in life, and he was looking forward to this new experience. All three sons did well adjusting to college life, for which I'm so thankful. This, of course, made it easier for me to adjust to my empty nest.

What Now?

They all did well, but I struggled with my own life, asking myself, "What do I do now?" I was a little depressed. The house was empty and quiet. I had spent decades caring for my three sons. My whole lifestyle had changed. But then, I reminded myself I was still a young woman and had almost half of my life to live, Lord willing. The question was: Besides my work, what was I going to do with my time in my personal life?

My first answer was to pay more attention to my wonderful husband! When we were first married, I was a widow with three boys, and Richard was divorced with no children. When he married me, he walked into a ready-made family when the boys were only half-grown. He was wonderful in stepping into a father-figure role and did a fantastic job helping me finish raising the boys.

However, because there were always three little boys running around, Richard and I never had the opportunity for the honeymoon period most couples enjoy after they are married and before children come along.

So, It Began

Our empty nest (a misnomer, by the way, since my husband and I were still in our nest!) became an opportunity to embrace a different lifestyle from before. We ate when we wanted and what we wanted. We stayed out late or went to bed early. We slept in, took long walks, went to movies, or had dinner on the spur of the moment, and we watched whatever we wanted on TV. And we made love whenever we desired. Our empty nest became a "love nest!"

> Being empty nesters actually became a whole lot of fun as we transformed our relationship.

We no longer had to stay up waiting until one of the boys came home, fix all the foods they wanted to eat, keep our bedroom door closed for privacy, or be attentive to all their separate schedules and work our own schedules around theirs. We had more food in the fridge, a much smaller food bill, and more hot water. There weren't size 11 shoes littering the hall or their stuff spread out everywhere. We were actually living in an uncluttered home. Such freedom! We could hardly contain ourselves.

Being empty nesters actually became a whole lot of fun as we transformed our relationship in this new season of life, strengthened our marriage, and grew even closer to each other. We had much more time to be with friends who filled our nest occasionally, to work on projects, explore new hobbies, and spend more time in Bible study. And aside from our busy work schedules, we had more time to just be with each other.

> We had more time to just be with each other.

Of course, we missed our boys, don't get me wrong. But we knew they were safe, managing to achieve good grades, and in a good, thriving Christian environment. They all had good common sense and were growing and maturing as they should. We had some hiccups, as all families do, but overall, college was a great experience for everyone.

They're Back!

When they came home from college for their summers, we had another challenge. Yes, they had grown up in many ways, but they still needed to heed to the house rules we had established. In our opinion, we asked very little. They still had a curfew, but a much later one than when they were in high school, of course. We asked them to let us know when they would be out and if they would not be home for dinner. They still needed to make their beds, clean up after themselves, and do their own laundry, which they had learned before going off to college. And they still were expected to attend church.

Of course, all three of them balked at some of these house rules at different times, but then I reminded them of whose house they were living in and who was paying for their food and for their opportunity to attend college. That quieted them. Since they are older now, I think they would agree we were fair as parents.

Flying Away

Launching our kids into the real world and becoming empty nesters was a hard season to find ourselves at times. I found it bittersweet, as I had to accept that our children were growing older. I realized it was imperative to their well-being and happiness, and to mine. Having a thirty-year-old across the breakfast table still at home and expecting me to finance them and mother them is not what I consider a healthy situation. So, just like the mother bird, I learned to let them go and fly on their own.

> I learned to let them go and fly on their own.

Sometimes, this meant pushing them out of the nest. One of our sons had been out on his own for a short time, and things job-wise and financially weren't working out for him at the time. He called and asked if he could come back and live for a while until he figured out his life. Well, of course, we said yes. What we didn't do was set some ground rules, and most importantly, we didn't define what "a while" was going to look like! He ended up very comfort-able and was still living with us after more than a year.

He obviously liked the no-cost living and the home-cooked meals. We finally had to set a deadline for him to find a place to live and told him he needed to move out. This was very tough love but necessary. However, after moving out, he realized he could do life on his own and matured greatly.

Finding Purpose

There have been many hope-filled events over the years since the boys all left our nest. My midlife became meaningful and purposeful. After much prayer, I began to find God's purpose in this new season of life. I was able to start and lead a women's Bible study, which then led to mentoring many women, which led to my creating a workshop to teach other women how to mentor, and finally, to my writing a book on mentoring. I realized there was much life to live after raising my children, a life of fulfillment and doing work for the Lord. I developed a meaningful life where I found purpose and identity, not just as my husband's wife, or my son's mom, or the boss's employee.

> I developed a meaningful life where I found purpose and identity.

Since we were not paying for three now men living in our home, and especially for college tuition anymore, we had more money and have been blessed to be able to travel. This has been a joy for both of us since we are adventurers at heart.

We have seen many new places, hiked many mountains, learned to play pickleball, and played golf regularly. We lead and host a couple's life group through our church and have had the opportunity to mentor many couples in their marriages. We facilitate the GriefShare (me) and DivorceCare (my husband) programs. So it has been very rewarding to know we are being used by the Lord in these ways.

We are living out the verse that says, "He comforts us in all our troubles so that we can comfort others. When they are troubled, we will be able to give them the same comfort God has given us" (2 Corinthians 1:4).

The Joy

Most importantly, after the sons left home and married, we now have the very best in life: grandchildren. Nothing beats being with our grands. We get to enjoy all the fun of parenting all over again without all the responsibilities. We just love them and play with them and then send them back to their parents.

My empty-nesting experience was an adjustment for me and a challenge at times, but I found it certainly wasn't the end of anything. It was the beginning of a new, exciting chapter in my life, a chapter I cherish, am proud of, thankful for, and enjoy immensely.

Navigating with Questions

MICHELLE RAYBURN

A T TIMES, THE NAVIGATION ON my phone sounds more like it's pondering life's mysteries than giving solid directions. Instead of straightforward instructions, the upward inflection at the end of every command often sounds like a question. Siri is the queen of uptalk. Not quite a Valley girl, but definitely a cousin.

"Turn left on County Road AA?"

"Merge into the right lane?"

"Keep left?"

It's as if it's asking, "Are you sure you want to get to your destination, or should we go on a scenic detour?"

Of course, I talk back. "Hey, Siri. Do you really know where we're going?"

"I'm sorry. I didn't get that. Continue for fifteen miles?"

We get caught in an awkward loop of question stacked upon question—Siri and me—each responding with another query. And still, with each uncertain turn, the destination becomes closer. I keep moving forward, pressing through the questions, knowing that inside of each one, there is a degree of certainty I must find and grasp.

If you don't typically ponder the intricacies of your phone's attitude, perhaps you can relate to this: navigating life as parents of adult children can feel decidedly uncertain—oxymoron intended. Questions stacked upon questions, theirs and mine. Sometimes mine go unspoken. Other times, they flow out in private conversations expressed only between the OC—original couple. I'll talk about that in a later chapter.

Should we just nod and smile as if we know what we're doing?

How can we support our adult child without being overbearing or intrusive?

Are they happy and fulfilled in their career and personal life?

Are they managing their finances responsibly? Do I want to know if they aren't? Is it any of my business?

How can I effectively communicate with them about a sensitive topic without causing conflict?

> One of the most challenging aspects is knowing when to step in and offer guidance.

One of the most challenging aspects is knowing when to step in and offer guidance and when to stand back and let them figure it out on their own. It's a delicate balance between wanting to shield them from life's hardships and allowing them the freedom to grow and learn from their experiences. Should we bite our tongues when we see them making what we perceive as awful mistakes, or is it our duty to intervene? Will we pay for those mistakes later by being the source to bail them out—literally, financially, or emotionally?

Countless parent-child relationships could be salvaged if we only knew the answers.

Detours and Signs

Questions turn up at every corner. Are we still responsible for their mistakes, or should we let them face the consequences of their actions independently? We can't send them to their rooms or ground them anymore. Taking away video games or car keys is no longer in our little bag of parenting tricks. So how do we handle the times when adulting isn't going so well?

> They will always need you—in different ways now.

How much advice is too much? Will they perceive our well-intentioned guidance as meddling and interference? Am I acting as a supportive parent or a helicopter one? Or a bulldozer one?

They come to us for help with the big stuff in life: car broke down on the side of the highway with no heat and a pregnant daughter-in-law inside. Septic backed up into the basement with putrid liquid dripping down—then gushing. The well made loud grinding noises and then went out. The furnace just made a sound like an explosion: "Is that bad?"

No matter the time of day, we answer those, still here when they need us. Perhaps you've heard it said that if you raise independent children who fly off with barely a glance backward, you've made yourself obsolete. Nothing could be further from the truth. They will always need you—in different ways now. You may know less about what they do every day, and you won't be baking them Barney or Big Bird cakes anymore, but you will never be obsolete.

And then there are the questions about their own precious offspring. What to do about a fever, a rash, constipation—yes, for the littles. How to handle tantrums—again, for the littles. They want us to have the answers like we did with their questions about how clouds are made or where water comes from.

It was easy to answer, "Do I have to go to school?"

"Yes."

But it isn't as easy to respond now. My replies often sound more like multiple-choice options. They're followed by more questions.

Despite our past perception of our parents' vast wisdom when *we* were the twenty-five-year-olds debating on whether to go to the ER, we now know older parents don't have all the answers. Sometimes my response comes out with Siri's inflection. "Yes?"

> There isn't always a perfect answer to offer.

There isn't always a perfect answer to offer.

In addition to all the questions swirling around being parents to our adult children, the process also means establishing some boundaries.

Twists and Turns

How do we maintain a healthy relationship with our adult children without overstepping our bounds? Should we wait for them to come to us with their problems, or should we initiate conversations about their lives? How often should we check in? More questions. I know. But it's a constant puzzle of determining when to offer a listening ear and when to respect their need for space.

One of our sons lives just a mile up the road from us. My husband often stops by to help with something, pick up a lawnmower or random car parts, or just to talk with our son for a few minutes.

One night, Phil arrived while their family was inside having supper. Their large windows gave the children a view of the yard from the table. We got a chuckle as they told the story of our little grandson's reaction to seeing his grandpa's red Chevy roll into the driveway.

"Grandpa's home!"

Yes, that's undoubtedly a sign that we might need to evaluate some boundaries.

Certain boundaries are easy: always texting before dropping in, keeping our mouths shut about parenting styles, and avoiding guilt-tripping, manipulation, or overly intrusive questioning. Others are a lot more difficult, downright blurry lines.

They're trying to figure it out too! Is it too soon to ask Mom and Dad to watch the kids again? Should we ask our parents for money?

Do we have to knock now when we come over to Mom and Dad's?

The answer to that last one is always no. This will forever be home base.

> The best way to process questions is through open conversations.

The best way to process questions is through open conversations. When in doubt, we assume the best about each other and communicate between the gaps. This mutual respect has blessed me so much. Our sons and our daughters-in-law are so respectful of my boundaries as a work-at-home freelancer. They honor the time I need to spend in my office.

We've talked through how to divide holiday time in a way that works for everyone. Of course, we're all far from perfect, but boundaries are for all of us—both ways.

New Roads

There's a shift beginning to take place in our family. We're approaching the phase of life where we begin to need their help more—not for the little stuff like dishes or mowing. For the big stuff. Like health crises. In this phase, the question becomes, "How do we ask *them* for help?"

I recall the day when my husband woke up in a terrible state of vertigo. Eventually, I wasn't even sure it was vertigo, and I knew he needed to get to the ER for evaluation. But he was lying on the bathroom floor and couldn't move an inch without the room spinning and inducing vomiting. I called our son who lives up the road.

Of course, I started crying as soon as he answered, which is *not* something we should do to our kids. "I need to you to come over and help me get Dad into the car to go to the hospital."

After the whole ordeal and an overnight stay in the hospital for Phil, our son admitted, "I see my future flashing before my eyes."

Yes, this was a painful glimpse at what might be to come. And I know now why it's hard for my own parents to ask me for help.

> Parenting adult children is a journey with more questions than answers.

Adjusting the Course

Ultimately, parenting adult children is a journey with more questions than answers. It's about adapting to new roles, learning to let go, and trusting that the foundation we've laid will guide them through life's maze, even when the path ahead seems uncertain.

Maybe we should ask an expert. "Hey, Siri. What should we do?"

The answer is sure to be another question. But I know we'll be all right. Are you with me?

Growing up Along the Way

LISA-ANNE WOOLDRIDGE

THE OPEN MAIL SAT IN a stack on my desk, next to two teacups and a large assortment of colorful pens. Next to them, several color-coded calendars gathered dust. My stash of sticky notes was missing, and the "Remember!" whiteboard was reduced to a short grocery list and a half-rubbed-off inspirational quote.

What was once my command center was now just another surface I needed to clean off. There were no more kids' schedules to input, activities to plan, or events to coordinate.

Being the family planner and organizer had always been a labor of love. Need two dozen cookies the morning of the bake sale? I'll pull a rabbit out of my hat. Need ideas for a book report? I've got suggestions coming out of my ears. Can't find your shoes/favorite sweater/science project? Just ask. I have a mental list of everything. I'm *on it*, whatever it is.

My family kept me hopping, shopping, and dropping. Chauffeur, administrative assistant, chef, nurse, counselor, personal shopper, teacher, field trip chaperone, you name it, I loved it. I had other jobs—meaningful work that I loved—that allowed me to interact with and minister to many people. And I had hobbies enough to make my husband despair every time I "popped" into the craft store.

Falling Down Memory Lane

I flipped through each calendar before I tossed it into a box. I had several years' worth of calendars on my shelf that I couldn't bear to part with—records of happy days spent at the lake with picnics, camping beneath towering redwoods, and swimming under our local waterfall brought me comfort. They reminded me I'd done the things I set out to do.

As a young parent, I was determined to make childhood as magical as possible for my children with campfires at the beach, stargazing parties with friends, and road trips to see what wonders we could find. I created treasure hunts with clues, hikes, and lots of cool loot to dig up. I turned ordinary stones into bejeweled dragon's eggs that hatched magical stuffed animals.

> I worked hard to give them stories to pass down and traditions to share with their own families someday.

I worked hard to give them stories to pass down and traditions to share with their own families someday. My own childhood was full of trauma and pain, so I was desperate to get it right for my children and not repeat the mistakes of the past. Raising happy, healthy children became my focus and goal.

It wasn't all sunshine and roses though. We often faced steep challenges and ailments that threatened to derail our lives altogether. It was a struggle from the start with premature babies, special needs diagnoses, and health challenges. There were years when we seemed to spend more time at the children's hospital than at home. We learned to trust God for pretty much everything—it's not as hard as it seems when you have no other choice. I made up for the hardships as best I could while working on my own health and inner healing. I made it the great work of my life, with God's help, to make my children feel safe and loved. My calendars reflected that attempt, all marked up in multi-colored, glittering gel pen ink. That was the reason I'd never thrown any of them away.

So why was I feeling so melancholy? I knew I was dragging my feet, not wanting to let go of a season that had defined most of my adult life. I had all the usual worries, most of which boiled down to, "Will my kids be okay?" Even with reminders of all the wonderful things we'd done, my calendars also had a lot of blank spaces.

Where did the time go? Had I wasted precious days with my kids when I should have given them a better education, or put them in more sports, or done more Bible studies? I was entrusted with them, but was I mindful enough of my own shortcomings? Had I trained them up in the way they should go? Had I failed them in some unknown way that would harm their future?

> I was afraid my inadequacies were more than my determination could overcome.

I'd struggled to recover from my own childhood. I'd come so far but was still insecure in my ability to be a good parent. I was afraid my inadequacies were more than my determination could overcome.

Lighting the Path

I knew enough to stop clearing things away and take a clear look at my feelings. Experience has taught me that when I'm avoiding something or being overwhelmed with sadness, it's time to sit down and ask for clarity, direction, and peace. Still, my inner critic piped up to chastise me. *Darn it, Lisa-Anne, if you would just keep up with your regularly scheduled spiritual maintenance appointments, your "check engine" light wouldn't be coming on when you're trying to do something else!*

Ignoring the negative self-talk, I launched straight into prayer without the usual preambles or formalities.

> Ignoring the negative self-talk, I launched straight into prayer.

"You know I tried. I wanted them to grow up in a family where they felt seen, and cherished, and even delighted in. I really didn't want to let the things that hurt me hurt them! Did I fail them? Did I fail you? I tried not to let my childhood wounds keep me from being a parent who modeled love and forgiveness and gentleness and mercy. I'm sorry if I messed it all up. I wanted to be a good mother, the way you're such a good Father." Tears slid down my face as I waited, whimpering into the ether.

Almost immediately, my words were turned back on me accompanied by a flood of images from my childhood.

"Was I a good Father?" I saw myself wrapped in a blue-checkered blanket, crying my heart out as a little girl. I remembered that despair clearly—and how God reminded me of his promise that weeping might spend the night, but joy would surely come in the morning (Psalm 30:5, paraphrased). I'd held on to that passage for years.

Other images passed through my mind, reminding me that no matter how dark things were, he'd never left me on my own. His comfort and consolation kept me going and saved my life in so many ways. I was filled with gratitude for his presence in my life from my earliest memories.

"Am I not still a good Father?" I felt the question probing the knot of fear that still gripped my heart.

Before I could answer, more memories made their way to the surface, but I was seeing them from the outside and not from my own eyes. It was like watching family movies in my mind. I saw myself going to the beach with friends, eating fun snacks, playing in the waves, then in the forest, staring in wonder at the huge redwood trees. I saw myself playing in waterfalls and splashing the kids, showering them with hugs and kisses, and whispering of God's love in their little ears. I saw my wonderful husband, the kindest and best man I've ever known, swinging the children in the air with me as we held their hands and walked through a majestic meadow in the shadow of a mountain.

> The tenderness and fierce love I felt for my children was an overflow of the tenderness and love I was receiving.

Understanding cascaded through me. God didn't just cut me off when I turned twenty-one, expecting me to be fully mature and able to handle come-what-may. He was taking me on field trips and giving me snacks and letting me rest in places of astounding beauty. The tenderness and fierce love I felt for my children was an overflow of the tenderness and love I was receiving, but not always perceiving, from him. He was still raising me while I was raising my children. And he was there for them in all the ways they'd needed him too.

Picking up the Trail

I picked up the last "Kid Calendar" on my desk and hugged it to my chest. It wasn't as full as some of the ones from years before, but I boxed it up with the others to be pulled out and pored over again someday. Maybe my kids would want some ideas for kids of their own. In the meantime, I'm starting a new calendar to book some fun activities for myself and my husband. It seems even adults benefit from field trips and snacks!

Wherever we go, wherever our kids go, I know the path has been prepared for us to walk in, and God will continue, every single day, to be a very good Father to us all. You can put that in glittery ink on your calendar.

Rock-a-Bye Renewal

PAM WHITLEY TAYLOR

HUGGED MY EIGHTEEN-YEAR-OLD SON, BEN, tightly as I said goodbye. Then I watched as he hopped into his loaded-to-the-brim Honda and drove away, college-bound to his freshman year—all by himself.

As a mom, I'd dreamed of that day that Ben would leave for college, and it certainly did not look like this. I'd imagined my hubby and me following Ben's Honda to his new school, helping him settle into his dorm, and taking him out to lunch to celebrate his new season. I'd envisioned picking up other things he needed for his dorm room and helping him get all settled in. Instead, as he drove away alone, I sat down in the middle of the floor and cried.

"Lord, it isn't supposed to be like this."

Mike, my sweet husband, was self-employed, and the oil well he was drilling was at a crucial point, so he had to stay on site. I, on the other hand, was running a critical care home hospital in the middle of our den.

Ben's younger disabled sister, Jan, had just come home from a fifty-day near-death summer stay at Baptist Hospital. Her doctors allowed her to go home early only because I'd learned to operate her new feeding pump, give her meds through that tube, and change her bandages. An IV pole held the pump and stood beside our old, oversized leather rocker where Jan and I spent much of our day. On the floor beside it was a suction machine that was frequently needed as Jan coughed and choked, and in the chair was a sheep skin that made it easier on Jan's thin skin when she sat up while I did housework or fixed meals. I rocked her much of the day to keep her calm. At this moment, her health was very fragile, and her needs were critical.

> I rocked her much of the day to keep her calm.

I adored my children and wanted desperately to always be there for both. This moment in time, however, seemed unfair in my eyes—especially to Ben. He had always adored Jan and seemed to understand the many times her care overshadowed his needs. He never complained about it.

A Heavy Heart

After my pity party/cry-a-thon following the early morning good-bye, I sat down and wrote a poem. Writing is how I have always coped with my hard places—I jot down my feelings on paper. Somewhere among my collection of multiple notebooks, that poem still exists, but I can't find it.

From my memories, I think it went something like this:

> How can I let go of this precious child I've birthed,
> this one who is flesh of my flesh
> and so dear to my heart?
> How can I send him off by himself?
> How can I handle all these goodbyes that are coming?
> Oh Lord, give me courage,

and in my absence, watch over Ben.
May this crooked path be made straight for him,
and, Lord, please protect him.
Give him a special blessing.
And, Lord, why does it have to be so hard?

And then I cried a bit more.

It would be another three years before our nest was actually empty, and it came with a very difficult decision. Jan had become disabled when she suffered brain damage during open heart surgery at only eight days of age. The failed surgery left her forever like a two-to-six-month-old infant, but as we and others prayed, Jan developed a precious little-kid personality and giggled and laughed and enjoyed life despite the multiple confines she faced.

> It would be another three years before our nest was actually empty.

She was delightful, and when she was well, she attended a school for special needs children. She seemed totally oblivious to her limitations. That was certainly a blessing. The problem now was her teenage body was growing, and her mama's was not.

The list of her meds and the schedule were stuck on our refrigerator door with a magnet. I slept when she slept. Before the feeding tube became necessary, I'd boiled her food weekly, ground her broccoli, chicken, and veggies, and kept them frozen and ready to fix for each meal. I still changed her diapers and kept her beloved music tapes playing beside her, and now my forty-three-year-old body struggled to meet her growing needs.

In a season of praying for God's direction, I learned of a wonderful pediatric care center only five miles from our home. Upon visiting it, peace filled my heart. By that fall, Jan entered that facility, and overnight, we became empty nesters. That unexpected and sudden empty nest left me grieving deeply.

But God is always so faithful to provide for his children in ways we can't imagine, especially when we have no idea what we need or what would help our grieving hearts.

A Healing Balm

A few weeks after Jan's placement, a new couple visited our church. I was drawn to them, not only because they had a new baby, but because the mama looked so tired. The dark circles under her eyes were deep.

I learned they'd just moved to Oklahoma from New Orleans. In fact, she shared that they were still unpacking. When I asked where they lived, I was astonished to find that not only did they live in our neighborhood, but they lived at an angle across the street from us. Their front door was visible from our front door. After asking a few more questions, I realized we'd been out of town visiting Ben at college when their moving van arrived.

A day or two after our meeting, I baked cookies and took them over late one afternoon. It was still a hard time of the day for me, and doing something for someone else always helped my heart.

I rang the doorbell, and my tired new friend answered with a sweet smile on her face and a crying baby on her hip.

> I *so* wanted to help, and I practically begged her to let me.

She stood among numerous unpacked boxes. Two of her young grade-school children vied for help with homework as the baby still fussed loudly. On top of that, I could tell this frazzled mama was in the midst of cooking dinner. I *so* wanted to help, and I practically begged her to let me.

Thankfully, she said, "Okay. It *would* help if you'd rock the baby for a little. She really needs a nap, and I can finish cooking dinner."

And then she did something amazing, she pointed me toward their rocking chair. Only God knew that snuggling and rocking baby Rachel was something my grieving heart desperately needed. After all, I had rocked Jan her entire life because it comforted her. Day and night—I had rocked her for sixteen years. We'd worn out one leather chair and were on the second one.

> I needed the joy and warmth of rocking a baby to help heal my heart.

But, as I grieved Jan's placement, I would have never guessed that I needed the joy and warmth of rocking a baby to help heal my heart. I rocked baby Rachel numerous times in the days that ensued, and even though it calmed her fussing, it was me who was most comforted each time.

A Hopeful Future

As I continued to heal, I also witnessed that a fresh pair of caregivers every eight hours, twenty-four hours a day, was amazing for Jan. After she'd been at the facility for a few months, her health improved. And to think, I'd thought no one could take as good of care of her as I did.

As Jan grew stronger, I did too. I still remember the day in the spring when I was able to leave town, drive to Ben's college dorm, and take him to lunch. He was a junior in college, and it was my first time to do that.

Today, as I write this story, my son, Ben, is fifty-one years old. He and his sweet wife have four grown boys and will soon be empty nesters themselves. I am so blessed to see what a strong husband and father Ben has become. He is deliberate in having special times with his family and does so many special things with each son—he does the things we couldn't do with him.

God certainly heard my prayers on that long-ago day when I watched that Honda drive away. He has made Ben's crooked way straight and blessed him. God has taught this mama to trust in him. And Jan, the little girl doctors said couldn't live past three, lived to be twenty-eight and spread her joy and love far beyond her family. My emptied nest was necessary because many great blessings followed it.

When Did the Oven Break?

MICHELLE RAYBURN

T HIS SEEMS TO BE TAKING a long time," Phil said as he fiddled with the temperature knob on the oven.

"You still didn't put that pizza in?" I said.

"I'm waiting for it to preheat."

"Well, it's been at least forty-five minutes, hasn't it?"

"Yep, and I'm hungry," he said.

"The oven doesn't take more than fifteen minutes to reach four hundred. Something is wrong."

We both paused for a moment, contemplating.

"When did we use it last?" he said.

"Huh. I have no idea. Was it when I baked those cookies? No. That was two weeks ago."

"I made bars last Thursday," he said. "Come to think of it, they didn't get done right. And something smelled weird."

We both burst out laughing. These two empty nesters had no idea when we'd last used our oven or when it malfunctioned. We give the toaster oven and air fryer regular workouts, but the oven not so much. There was a time in our childrearing years when the oven seldom got a break. Between baking five loaves of bread each week, making meals, and baking treats, I couldn't have gone fifteen minutes without knowing the bottom element had gone out.

New Reality

When our sons lived at home, I made homemade meals, and we all sat at the table together every night. Lest you think I have some sort of food snobbery going here, the homemade meals happened mostly because I could feed a family of four on the cheap by shopping at Aldi and cooking at home. We also had a vegetable garden. I had made it my purpose to figure out how to keep the bank account balanced on Phil's one full-time income and a little pocket change I earned from teaching piano lessons.

> The basement cellar has been purged of discolored jars of applesauce and stewed tomatoes—the remnants of overambitious canning sessions.

Without two teenagers and their friends hanging around, our eating habits—and shopping habits—have gone through a dramatic transformation. It's been a while since we went through cereal by the truckload. The pantry doesn't need to be so packed with overstock that jars of peanut butter or boxes of snack bars tumble onto our heads when we open the doors. There is actually space in the big freezer, and the post-shopping game of Tetris to get the goods stashed is gone. I can effortlessly slip a bucket of caramel vanilla ice cream, frozen salmon, and a box of my husband's favorite Eggo waffles into the space.

The basement cellar has been purged of discolored jars of applesauce and stewed tomatoes—the remnants of overambitious canning sessions. No one makes enough chili or spaghetti to warrant the abundance I stocked every year of the garden harvest, much less two parents of grown children. Besides, fried eggs and pancakes come together much faster for a spontaneous supper than a pot of chili.

> You have permission to do whatever you wish.

No Rules

If for no other reason, I put this all here on paper for you to read between the lines. If you missed it, get this: you have permission to do whatever you wish. If fussing over recipes and ingredients and dishes to rival Julia Child's French cuisine revs up your joy, do it! If you hate to cook, find a different way. You've nurtured those babies and turned them into fine, sturdy stock. If the kitchen is closed and the oven is broken, turn off the negative self-talk and shoulds. This is your domain.

I cleared out two shelves in my kitchen by tossing and donating saved back issues of *Taste of Home* magazine and heaps of cookbooks. Yes, we kept a few favorite books. However, we're way more likely to cook with a phone in hand and a new recipe on the screen than to page through a museum of old books.

Those internet queries usually begin with things like "recipes that use sour cream, milk, and cream cheese." This is because we have to find creative ways to use up the things that expire when there are no boys willing to chug a quart of milk that's within thirty minutes from turning into cottage cheese.

New Routine

When our boys went to college, I wasn't sure I'd done the best job of teaching them what needed to be done in the kitchen. Or how to shop for groceries. But some of the most heartwarming conversations with them were when one would explain how he went to the local Market Foods and shopped for what was on sale in the flyer for that week. Or when another explained what creative meals he made from ingredients found for a bargain at Aldi.

Our youngest son eventually moved into an apartment with his college friends, and the guys started cooking meals together and eating at the table—family style. They became masters at using my castoff slow cooker for the wild game they hunted. They fried up the fish they caught and even experimented with homemade bread. Nearly a decade later, we hear that one of those friends still makes the whole wheat recipe for his family now.

> While our daily routines have simplified, family gatherings have taken on a new significance.

While our daily routines have simplified, family gatherings have taken on a new significance. When our sons, their spouses, and our grandchildren come over, the kitchen comes alive again. It's a wonderful chaos filled with the laughter and camaraderie that only family can bring. A daughter-in-law arranges fresh green beans and garlic on an oven tray for roasting. Another daughter-in-law chops a salad and tosses it with dressing. I mash potatoes and stir gravy while my husband carves a turkey. Every surface brims with the fixings, and the fridge bursts with bowls. We sometimes even use the bonus oven, the one used for canning, to roast a large turkey or bone-in ham out of the way.

We add all three expansion boards to the dining table and sit shoulder-to-shoulder to fit high chairs and booster seats. And after we run the dishwasher several times and scrub the pans, put it all away to be untouched until the next gathering, we send them home with takeout containers of leftovers. We cherish these moments, knowing that they arc now the exception rather than the rule.

When the house is quiet again, and we've reduced the table back to our new normal size and stowed the extra chairs, I'll flop on the sofa and put my feet up, smiling at the thought that I won't have to worry about feeding another person for a few days. Tomorrow, we'll scavenge the leftover bits of ham and mashed potatoes that we saved for ourselves.

The day after that, we'll have cheese and crackers or a simple salad. Popcorn can be a great supper. An omelet is easy. And when I'm in the mood to fire up that oven, we'll have a delicious, blackened salmon with roasted asparagus and a spinach salad topped with blackberries and vinaigrette—because we're not totally devoid of nutrition in our devoid nest—food our children would *never* have eaten when they lived at home. Of course, there will be some ice cream for a little scoop because it sticks around these days, right where I last left it in the freezer.

No Regrets

Our children have grown into capable adults, often hosting us in their own homes. It's a delight to see them navigate their kitchens, preparing meals and creating their own traditions. These visits are a reminder of the cyclical nature of life—how the skills and values we've passed on continue to thrive in the next generation.

> It's been fun to be guests at their tables and in their kitchens.

From chicken alfredo, to tacos, to Ethiopian food, it's been fun to be guests at their tables and in their kitchens. When we go away for a vacation together, they plan the meals, and I rent the VRBO. We can relax and play with the grandchildren while they worry about preparations, cooking, and cleanup.

Our days of frantic meal prep and endless grocery runs are behind us. We've moved from a life dictated by the needs of our growing boys to one that affords us the luxury of simplicity and spontaneity.

Life has a new rhythm, and we're dancing to it—content, adaptable, and grateful for every delicious moment it brings. Here's to the joy of savoring each season as it comes, one bite at a time.

Awkward Questions of the Empty Nest

MICHELE MORIN

ONE SPRING DAY, FLOOR PLANS and scholarship applications littered my dining room table. The talk around dinner was all about the future as one son was building a house, and another (the youngest!) was looking forward to graduation. Life as I knew it then was about to undergo a drastic change here on this country hill.[3]

Having homeschooled a brood of four sons for the past twenty-one years, I had certainly seen our story trending in this direction and had felt the current of life rushing toward the door. I had not missed the significance of the unpredictable number of place settings at dinner, the unexpected date nights when my good husband and I realized we were home alone—again!

One by one, my sons were growing and going with miles between us and full schedules that fully occupied their time and attention. Leisurely conversations over breakfast or dinner were gradually being replaced with the scratchy, distorted audio of over-the-road cell phone calls as they traveled on their way to work or class.

I remember that eventually, I became an object of concern to some since the "baby" had turned eighteen and was poised to graduate in the spring. They began to ask, tentatively, kindly, as if, perhaps, it might be a tender subject for me, "What on earth are you going to do with yourself?"

> One by one, my sons were growing and going with miles between us.

Awkward Questions

I'm used to questions. Although I did not realize it at the time, I have since noticed how unusual it is to schlep a shopping cart and four sons through a grocery store. "Are they all yours?" was the most common query I received in the season of the loaded blue minivan, but my favorite was the inappropriate and completely boundary-less, "Do they all have the same father?" (What...?)

One day, the awkward questions of the empty nest season coalesced in the dining room. I stood in this liminal space, holding a stack of blue and tan Pfaltzgraff and an indeterminate number of forks, when all the questions from all the seasons of my mothering life met and danced in a circle around my emptying nest.

I realized then, in a sense, that nothing had changed.

The duties are all still there: the food prep, the studying, the laundry, the teaching, the vacuuming, the long listening to friends. The proportions are all that differ. Even in the intense season of four daily math lessons and multiple sports and music drop-offs and pick-ups, I would have been found rummaging around in the Sermon on the Mount while parked outside the middle school. Even then, I persevered in scrawling lines into a well-floured notebook while rolling pie dough.

All the love is still there. Little hands still hold loaded paintbrushes and cut gingerbread boys from sticky dough at my kitchen counter, but they belong to my grandchildren now. The concerned phone calls, the proffered wisdom, and the checking-in now run in both directions, as our sons have surpassed us in many practical ways that include cleaning carburetors and making wise investments. Even so, they continue to do us the honor of asking our advice now and then. Band-Aids are no longer dispensed on the daily, but encouragement and help to the young women in my life feels a little bit like healing.

> They continue to do us the honor of asking our advice now and then.

My mothering life goes on, and this is surely what will lie at the center of whatever response I live my way into as an answer to every season's new line of questioning. When the house was perpetually noisy, when pizza was on the menu every Friday, and we argued over which Disney movie to pop into the VCR, I thought I would never forget any of it—I would remember it always just the way it was.

Answers Shaped by Love

With gratitude, I can report that the stories we tell one another about our family in the past have been molded by the shape of our family today. Funny stories become a better memory every year. Wrongs of the past, while still wrong and regrettable, have been so completely forgiven that the sting of the story has been swallowed up in love.

Maybe what author Madeleine L'Engle said of herself, looking back upon a full life, is also true of my family: "I am still every age that I have ever been."[4] The stages of a mothering life are built from a series of moments: now, now, and now quickly become then, and my family-as-it-is collides in memory with my family-as-it-was.

It's absolutely true that fear of the unknown, multiple and conflicting priorities, and the challenges presented by an aging body will all seem insurmountable at times as we move into the season of the empty nest. However, it is also true that when our dreams for the future are God-inspired, they will also be God-empowered. We are invited to take the risk and experience God's faithfulness firsthand.

As I look fondly in the rearview mirror of my personal history, I see a time when I was responsible for forty fingernails and forty toenails that were not my own. I lived a sandwich-making, T-shirt-folding life that required acres of pepperoni pizza and hundreds of miles in a minivan. While it is true that those days are behind me, it is also true that those days have changed me.

An action verb, mothering always has and will continue to comprise elements of giving and telling, listening, and nurturing. Mothers in every season are tasked with the creation of safe emotional spaces long after the need for clean socks and a full lunch box has expired.

> What story do I want to be able to tell going forward?

What in the world will I do with myself now that my boys have become young men and my mothering in the flesh is now, primarily, a mothering of the spirit? The answer, I believe, will be another question because it has been the question shaping my decisions and ordering my priorities all along: What story do I want to be able to tell going forward?

I'm trusting for grace to tell a story about how God enabled me to let go when it was time to let go—and to hold on with holy ferocity to the things that are still mine to do.

Holding on and Letting Go

I've discovered that it's not just the eight-passenger mini-van and the pile of mismatched socks that can go. Learning to thrive after our kids leave home means that we are moving toward freedom from many long-standing expectations and time-consuming traditions.

And, like it or not, once our kids take flight, we let go of control. We become observers from a place outside the center of their lives. We may get the memo about the new earring, the creative hair color, and the decision about facial hair or finances at the same time as the rest of the world.

> As children leave the nest, all that letting go frees our minds and our hands for new pursuits.

When I was teaching four math lessons a day and shuttling kids to music and sports, there was no way I could have boarded a plane and spent a weekend teaching women hundreds of miles down the East Coast. As children leave the nest, all that letting go frees our minds and our hands for new pursuits. I miss my kids, and it looks as if I'll never master the art of making less than six quarts of soup, spaghetti, or American chop suey. Still, those dinners of leftovers enjoyed alone with my husband in peace and quiet aren't a bad consolation prize.

Therefore, I'll hold on to new opportunities to minister to people outside my home circle. I'll hold on to the freedom to weed my garden without a baby monitor nearby, to meet friends for coffee occasionally, to work on my writing craft, to spend a half hour making notes on the thirty "I wills" in the book of Hosea while my second cup of tea cools.

I'm holding on to the small hands of grandchildren who love to come to Bam's house, where we paint, dig in the garden, read stories, and bake cookies together. All of life is a gift, and this season is no exception. While the steps are unfamiliar to me at this point, I'm discovering a certain excitement as I look around me at this empty nest and see the wide-open spaces of God's good plans for the future.

Finding Passion
and Purpose

Soul Clothes

KIM CUSIMANO

When it was time for you to go,
I had to stay.
Not alone.
Your old backpack hung around in the closet.
Your lacrosse stick stood guard in the garage.

Moments standing in dusty places,
With companions weathered and true.
Crying gentle tears in their secret company,
Like standing with whispering bones.

They had stories of their own.
Worn handles from years of helping you grow up.
Hours in classrooms,
Late nights on sports fields with lights.

Thankful a new day has come,
New friends have arrived.
Your college laundry basket burst through the door,
Like it owned the place.

Your roommate visiting for the weekend was such a delight.
Your own animated stories,
Funny and silly,
But strangely strong.

That basket of laundry,
Maybe it's my most relatable friend.
Carrying your wrinkled robe,
You wear it on lazy days.

Your favorite T-shirt,
That accessorizes all the fun.
And that college hoodie,
Announcing many dreams to come.

I guess my mom's heart has a basket,
Has my soul clothes,
My mood choices,
My wardrobe for my days.

I can dress my heart in sadness or joy.
I can pair memories with tears or chuckles.
I can treasure the past days,
Yet unbuckle the belt of mourning.

I can borrow your newfound adventure,
Try it on in my own size.
I can still dress up as Mom,
But also as your forever friend.

Like jewelry,
I can smile at your new stories,
I can laugh a belly laugh with you.
If you can wear your grown-up sparkle,
I can keep on sparkling too!

Adjust to Conditions

KOLLEEN M. LUCARIELLO

OOKING BACK ON MY YESTERYEARS, I recognize my obsession with planning. Depending on the day, I might have been mentally drafting my escape from parental control, my retreat from siblings who annoyed me, or what I now recognize as my feelings of inadequacy.

A Planner Must Plan

I am certain I was in elementary school when I opened the local newspaper and discovered the bridal section while visiting my grandparents on a Sunday afternoon. This day is forever etched in my memory. The display of women adorned in their bridal attire captivated me. I was a little girl incessantly dreaming about the day my face would be amid the presentation. I relished every opportunity to open this newspaper section for another chance to admire the brides. Enraptured by them, I would circle the picture of the bride I'd chosen to win *Prettiest on the Page*—the one I would someday become.

What I failed to realize at that young age was that when my time eventually arrived, adjustments would be made to whatever imaginings I had from those earlier days. I would choose the wedding dress that felt as though it was made *just for me*. My prince and I would do our best to plan the day that best represented us. And except for the polka band his parents hired to provide the music, it was a well-planned day that fit us. And it would be *our picture* that graced the pages of the paper from our special day in 1982.

Whoops! Who Planned for This?

With the wedding behind us, we set out for our new life as Mr. and Mrs. We envisioned countless opportunities to love, laugh, and adventure, which gave us plenty to plan and prepare for. We were both caught a bit off guard when, within a few short months, a positive pregnancy test interrupted our plan. This required quite an adjustment for us, as well as for a family member who found it challenging to embrace. I was only nineteen, after all, when we'd married, and now, I would become a mother at twenty. Nonetheless, even though we hadn't planned for parenthood, we were thrilled for God's gift of a son. Over the next few years, we'd become a family of five.

> Without fail, it seemed I'd just get settled into one season, and another one began to encroach upon me.

My days and plans soon revolved around baby or toddler needs. Feeding time, nap time, and bedtime became the dictators of *my time*—as did the three cherubs requiring them. Without fail, it seemed I'd just get settled into one season, and another one began to encroach upon me. Year after year, plans revolved around car-pools, school schedules, after-school activities, and sporting events. Family vacations and extended family gatherings were in the mix too. For twenty-four years, my plans had been intertwined with the plans of my three offspring and their father's work schedule.

The Shape of a Plan

Gretchen Rubin is credited with saying, "The days are long, but the years are short."[5] I would be delusional to deny how extremely long some days felt. I encountered a new attitude with every age and endured countless temper tantrums and power struggles.

Sometimes, they even came from the kids.

Periodically, my thoughts would set sail on a ship that would carry me to a distant land called Liberation. It would be here that I would wander about, pondering how my days would be spent when I was no longer responsible for the duties required of me as a stay-at-home mom. *What will I do with the time when I no longer need to run kids here, there, and everywhere?* I'd think to myself. "Anything I want," I would whisper back.

Failure to Launch

Then, one day, I woke up and realized that the long days had indeed become short years. My imaginings were no longer necessary to cruise me to the land of Liberation. The reality of life's seasons had swept me up and carried me there.

> I'd never planned or prepared myself mentally or emotionally for the reality of it.

The days following our baby boy's departure from the nest began to expose my lack of planning for the day this would happen. Sure, I'd dreamt of it. But I'd never planned or prepared myself mentally or emotionally for the reality of it. I could no longer drift happily over to Liberation. Instead, I was caught up in a stormy sea of conflict, confused with little self-confidence.

Shame began to take root within me when someone would ask, "What are you doing now that you have an empty nest?" "Are you going to get a *real* job?"

The answer that followed was usually, "I don't know." The insinuation that I hadn't held a "real job" as a stay-at-home parent began to echo within me and destroy my self-image. Yes, I'd held different jobs during the years my kids were in school, but I never sensed it was God's plan for me to find a full-time one now that they had moved on. My identity was challenged as I compared myself to others and became more concerned about what people thought of me.

> My identity was challenged as I compared myself to others and became more concerned about what people thought of me.

The storm was intense. We hear of children who fail to launch, but it would appear I was the one failing to launch. The turmoil consumed me until God adjusted my perspective while walking through the woods.

Behind our home is a trail leading to the town cemetery, and a little pond sits in the back corner of the cemetery. It's a short trek to a secluded area where our kids used to fish for nothing but believed they'd be able to hook a big one. I made my way to the pond, sat down in the lush, green grass, and began to ask God for direction. Just as softly as the breeze moved the leaves on the trees, a verse from Proverbs floated through my mind. "We can make our plans, but the LORD determines our steps" (16:9).

Okay, Lord, you have permission to determine my steps. Just please tell me what they are. And hurry. I prayed my days of hoping I could "catch a big fish when I was throwing my line into a fishless pond" were ending.

#beReconciled to God's Plan

If God was going to determine my steps, I needed to let him reinvent my life. And, for me, the Lord intended first to adjust my understanding of identity. Through my time in his Word, I recognized how I'd allowed my *who* to become swallowed up by my *do*. I was in the middle of a full-blown identity crisis because my identity had become so wrapped up in what I was doing or what others thought I should be doing. Resting and waiting for God's next assignment was nearly impossible.

The voice in my head I've nicknamed Messy Melinda constantly nagged, *"What will others think about you?"* This was a precise moment when I had to decide if I would do what *I thought* I should or what *God intended* for me to do. There's a difference. One thing was evident: I would no longer be defined by my *do*.

Step by step, year by year, my life has transformed because my identity has been remade. Some steps were taken with knees knocking as I fought nerves that were anything but steel. It felt utterly unnatural to put my life on pause when the entirety of it had been packed full of busyness. It wasn't easy to be still and not allow this season of dormancy to push me into a commitment that would keep me busy and possibly with the motive to appease others. Jesus knew exactly who he was and what his Father had planned for him. I wanted that too.

> Who I believe I am in Christ awakens within me a spiritual truth that brings clarity, confidence, and worth.

Who I believe I am in Christ awakens within me a spiritual truth that brings clarity, confidence, and worth into my life. It took some therapy to help me adjust to a new approach in my thinking. And if I can embrace how he defines me, I will no longer be shaken by the approval ratings of others. The reality is that people will wound you with their words in the here and now. However, we can and must live by this truth: they will never define you by them. Unless you let them. Please don't ever let them. He's always for you, and he always adores you.

A God-Shaped Plan

God used a beautiful psalm of David to tell me where I was during my lost and lonely days. "I waited patiently for the LORD to help me, and he turned to me and heard my cry. He lifted me out of the pit of despair, out of the mud and the mire. He set my feet on solid ground and steadied me as I walked along" (Psalm 40:1–2).

The day at the pond was the beginning of a new journey with him and a new season for me. Step by step, I found him faithful to steady me as I walked along, and he adjusted me to the new conditions of a kingdom identity. Oh sure, I have moments when I forget that I no longer need to justify myself to Messy Melinda. He began to reveal purpose and invited me to step into his plan for me to start writing. I never knew I could write. Had I known, I might have put more effort into my high school English class assignments.

> He began to reveal purpose and invited me to step into his plan.

He would also release me to step out to build the woman's ministry he'd planted within my heart decades before. I only needed to make space for him, wait on his timing, and reconcile myself to my *true* identity—the one he gave me when he knew me before all time. You can too. It's here, in this place, that you were always meant to be.

Zipping In and Out of the Empty Nest

ROBYN MULDER

WITH A NAME LIKE ROBYN, I've always liked the imagery of nests. After I married Gary in 1990, we began filling our little nest with children. By the year 2000, we had four little birds: Erin, Allison, Blake, and Dylan. It got a bit crowded at times as all of us jostled around together and experienced the ups and downs of life.

But then our nest began to empty out. First, Erin flew off to college and a teaching job in Iowa. A year later, Allison fluttered off to college. Then she landed back at home for a year or so while deciding what she wanted to do. Blake winged his way to the same college and soared as a theater major. He also returned to the nest for a time before finding a job he wanted. Finally, Dylan left home and went to school. He also hopped back after graduation and spent some time with us before venturing out on his own.

Eventually, all four of our little birdies ended up in Lincoln, Nebraska, after our oldest daughter started teaching elementary school there. Our nest is empty, and we're again adjusting to being a family of two.

I Wanted This, Didn't I?

Even though I sometimes resented the seemingly constant demands on my time while our kids were young, I've been surprised to miss those days now that our nest is empty. I thought I would do so much with my free time once the kids flew the coop, but it's been a struggle to find a sense of balance now that they're all gone. It's only been a couple of years, so I suppose I'm still in that adjustment period, trying to find a new rhythm in life now that my days belong mostly to me.

> I've been surprised to miss those days now that our nest is empty.

I suppose most women go through the same feelings after their last child leaves home. Without children to care for, our lives sometimes become rather boring as we settle into a personal routine that can feel like we're just going through the motions if we aren't careful. Routine is good, but we need to plan moments of fun and novelty if we really want to enjoy life.

Trying Something New

While attending a writing conference in California recently, a group of us decided to go zip-lining high in the redwoods of Mount Hermon Camp and Conference Center. I had brought up the idea after walking under the zip lines the previous two years while I was at the conference. It looked like fun, and I wanted to try it!

Once our group was strapped into our harnesses and helmets, I started to change my mind. Our guides helped us maneuver a short zip line about ten feet off the ground. "Maybe we should just do that six times," I jokingly suggested. The guides laughed, and then they led us to a long, bouncy bridge that got us up to the first platform. It was 150 feet high, but we didn't know that until later.

My friends and I looked at each other nervously as our guides clipped and unclipped our straps as we moved from the bridge to the platform around a tall redwood. Did we really want to do this?

> I stepped down onto the platform and then took another step, and I was off!

When our guide asked who wanted to go first, I raised my hand. Might as well get it over with, I reasoned. I shook a bit as I took a couple of steps up and got my trolley clipped onto the line. I put one hand on top, as instructed, and grabbed a strap with my other hand. I stepped down onto the platform and then took another step, and I was off!

I loved it and enjoyed every moment of our zip-lining adventure.

Zip-lining Got Me Thinking about Our Nest

As I flew through the air on each of the six zip lines that day, I wasn't thinking about much besides following our guides' instructions and having fun. But after the experience was over, I started to make some comparisons to my empty nest and thought of each of my children.

Some of our kids would probably love an experience like this, while others would rather stay on the ground and watch. Honestly, I felt a bit of fear come over me as I thought about one of my kids going on the zip line. It would be more difficult to watch them plunge off the edge of a high platform than it was for me to do it myself.

Life Can Sometimes Feel Like a Zip Line

All of us have challenges that come our way from time to time. Sure, we have our normal routines, and those can feel pretty comfortable most days. When we decide to try something new, it can feel scary.

Like stepping out into thin air, we wonder if we'll succeed at a new experience or if we'll fall flat on our faces.

Watching our children go through life, far from the safety of the nest they grew up in, can feel even more frightening. Will they fly? Or will they fail?

In or Out, Learning to Trust

Now that our kids are out on their own, I have to trust that they'll be okay. God loves them even more than I do, and he'll take care of them. I don't have to be afraid as I watch them try new things. They just might fall (hopefully not 150 feet!), but they'll learn from those failures and become stronger people as a result.

It's time for me to let go of my little brood and focus on my own adventures. Sometimes I can lounge around the nest and relax, enjoying the trinkets I've collected over the years. I have a room full of craft supplies where I can create handmade cards for family members and friends. My desk is perfect for journaling and completing writing projects as well as editing for other writers. Our kitchen is just right for cooking and baking delicious meals and snacks.

Our home is a comfortable place, even if the location changes once in a while. (My husband is a pastor, so we've moved six times since we got married.) There is plenty to keep me busy: writing, editing, volunteering at church and in the community, and visiting those precious grandchildren. I suppose I wouldn't ever have to go far from my nest if I didn't want to.

But there are things I want to do that will take me zipping out of the nest. I want to travel, challenge myself to learn new things, and attempt to accomplish big goals. That's scary! It takes trust—trust in God and trust in myself.

When I went zip-lining, I put complete trust in the harness and straps that were keeping me attached to the cable stretched high up in the trees. Without that sense of trust, I wouldn't have been able to relax and enjoy myself.

> I want to travel, challenge myself to learn new things, and attempt to accomplish big goals.

I could never have stepped off those platforms if I had been afraid something might break every time. I also had lots of faith in our guides. They knew what they were doing as they clipped and unclipped our equipment. They warned us about ways we could get hurt if we didn't follow their instructions. Still, they also suggested ideas to ramp up the experience and have even more fun—like "walking the plank" and going off backward.

As I go through life, I'm slowly learning that it's vital to put complete trust in God so I can really enjoy life. Without that trust, I'm too often afraid I'm going to fall. That fear keeps me huddled up in my nest, unwilling to fly. God upholds me. He warns me about ways I could get hurt if I don't follow his instructions. But he also encourages me to be daring and try some things I never would have contemplated on my own.

Isaiah 40:31 says, "But those who trust in the LORD will find new strength. They will soar high on wings like eagles. They will run and not grow weary. They will walk and not faint." When we trust God completely, we don't have to be afraid. We can zip in and out of our empty nests and enjoy the lives God has given us.

Caregiving at Any Age

KELLY WILSON MIZE

A S I SAT PLUCKING AWAY at the computer, two cuddly cats played at my feet. They jumped up and pranced dangerously close to the keyboard, blocking the screen, vying for my attention. As I desperately struggled to focus on my work, I realized the scene seemed somehow familiar. And then I remembered.

In my mind, I traveled back to a time when two tiny humans also used to play at my feet while I worked. My eyes clouded with tears as I remembered those days: the best years of my life and yet also some of the most trying. The saying, "The days are long, but the years are short," could not be more true. There is nothing quite like being a parent—the experience reveals in us a perfect mixture of the most intense emotions—beautiful, heart-wrenching, and profound. The assignment is not for the faint of heart.

The Right Place for Me

When my children were preschoolers, the world was a different place. There were no smartphones, and there was no social media. My circle of stay-at-home moms would commiserate about breastfeeding woes and potty training via a landline phone—in solidarity with other moms at home with young children. Thankfully, there were Bible studies and Mother's Day Out programs, blessed picnics at the park, and fun playdates on the Chick-fil-A playground. But many days, I was home alone with my kids, and honestly, there were times I felt terribly lonely. One particular day is etched in my memory. I stepped outside to play with my kids on a beautiful, warm day, looked up and down my eerily quiet street, and felt like we were the only three living things on earth.

> How am I supposed to change the world if I can't even leave the house at naptime?

I would ask God almost daily, "Is this what I am supposed to be doing with my life? I love my kids more than anything and want the best for them, but is this it? How am I supposed to change the world if I can't even leave the house at naptime?"

It wasn't necessarily what I wanted to hear and may not have come directly from the mouth of God, but the answer always came—again and again, clear as a bell. *Your life may not be glamorous or rewarding in the way that society rewards, but you are exactly where you are supposed to be. Motherhood is the most important job in the world.*

I toyed with the idea of going back to work when my kids were small, but with no family in town, the thought of paying a stranger to watch them seemed to cancel out many of my reasons for getting a job in the first place. Thankfully, I discovered opportunities to write. My children, if not playing at my feet, were never far away. Having the option, financially, to be able to stay home with them was a blessing I did not take for granted. I have many friends, though, who continued to work outside the home throughout their children's upbringing who were, and are, excellent mothers. But my husband and I realized it just wasn't the right decision for our family at that time.

Special Visits

During those preschool years, one welcome distraction outshined all other social events and brightened many days. Grandparent visits were a treat for us all. My parents, retired and living a couple of hours away, were playmates like no other. The kids and I looked forward with great anticipation to their visits every few weeks. On the days they made the trip, I was every bit as excited as the children to see their grandparents' car pull into the driveway. They would take us to lunch, entertain the kids for a few hours, and give me a short break from the monotony of everyday life. My parents played an active role in helping me get through that sometimes challenging season of motherhood.

I now look back on those years as some of the most fulfilling of my life. But as with many parents, when I think back to the time my children were small, I wish I had taken more time to truly absorb the wonder of their childhoods. Because before I knew it, the sweet toddlers playing at my feet were no longer. Seemingly overnight, they morphed into children. The playdates at the park were replaced with homework, endless sports practices, and busy social calendars.

After my kids started school, I revisited the question of my "life's purpose" daily and eventually decided to return to work, teaching at the school they attended. Those quiet days at home quickly vanished into thin air, and as the children became teens, it was sometimes hard to even remember how things had once been.

And then one day, just like that, they were grown.

New Roles

My children have blossomed into successful young adults. When they were younger, I always thought my job as a parent would be complete when they moved out of my house and into the world, but I could not have been more wrong! They are twenty-three and twenty-five as I write, and I still reminisce every day, worry about them, pray for them, and constantly consider how I could have parented them better when they lived under my roof. They are always on my mind, even though I no longer have any control over any aspect of their lives.

Soon after my youngest graduated from high school, I retired from the classroom. But I am blessed with freelance writing assignments and continue to spend many days—like before—tapping away at my computer, with cats at my feet where toddlers used to be.

> How can I change the world now that I've gotten so old?

In this strange new season, like many times before, I find myself asking God, "What am I supposed to be doing with my life? Is this it? How can I change the world now that I've gotten so old, and my experience and ideas seem so outdated and irrelevant?"

But as I sit with the cats at my feet, a familiar answer comes. Once again, it may not be glamorous or rewarding in the way that society rewards, but I realize I am in a good place–with a flexible schedule that allows me to be available at a moment's notice to help my grown children when they need me. But also for another very important reason. I am thankful to have the opportunity to help care for my aging parents—the two people who have loved and cared for me throughout every stage of my life so far.

As I write, my dad is ninety, my mom is close behind him in age, and they are still living independently, but just barely. We all realize there will be major changes soon. They themselves have been empty-nesting for a whopping thirty-five years now, and just when they perfected that role, they are beginning to experience another sobering life transition—from parents back, in many ways, to children. My position as a caregiver has been reversed and reimagined. I have shifted from caring for those to whom I gave birth to caring for those who gave birth to me.

> My position as a caregiver has been reversed and reimagined.

I try to visit my parents weekly, knowing my time with them is limited. I am doing my best to help them in any way I can as they face this challenging final season of life.

The tables have turned.

Nostalgic Return

These days, *they* look forward to *my* visits with great anticipation. They couldn't be happier to see my car turn into the driveway. I bring lunch, entertain them for a few hours, and give them a break from the monotony of everyday life. I return home—to their home—no longer thinking of my own identity as an empty nester but arriving as the aging bird-child that flew away from *their* nest so long ago. And I realize that they have spent endless days, as I have with my grown children, reminiscing, worrying about me, praying for me, and constantly considering how they could have parented me better.

I assure them that they did just fine.

So, when I feel sad or nostalgic about my own empty nest, I think about theirs. I realize that history does in fact repeat itself, from generation to generation, and that one day soon, my husband and I will be in my parents' shoes.

There is nothing quite like being a parent. Precious babies grow to be children, then teens, and then one day the cherished birds fly away from the nest to begin the process all over again, forging their own futures, and taking with them all that their parents have worked so hard to teach.

But for the very fortunate, the grown-up children return again and again as often as they are needed, remembering that for caregiving at any age, "The days are long, but the years are short." May we all, and every generation to come, be attentive in caring for those who have been there for every season of our lives and have indeed taught us everything we know.

Launching Books and Young Adults

LYNETA SMITH

OW CAN ONE TINY PERSON create such a big ruckus?" When I held my firstborn daughter, Mariah, in my arms that first day together in the hospital, I marveled at how this tiny miracle had upended my whole world. For the life of me, I could not have imagined letting her go to kindergarten, let alone to college. I wanted to snuggle her for the rest of my days, swaddling her chubby little legs and inhaling that new baby smell. I'd keep her here forever.

Fifteen years later, I nearly changed my mind when several daily outfit changes replaced swaddling blankets and tiny socks. But at fifteen, it was high time for her to learn how to do this basic skill herself, so I introduced my hesitant home economics student to the laundry room and showed her how to run the washer.

You can't blame her for resisting, what with her full schedule and all. She kept busy cleaning her own room, doing assigned schoolwork, and spending hours in front of the mirror. Not a lot of time for washing and drying her own clothes.

Out of nowhere, she burst into tears. "You just want me to learn how to do this so I'll be able to leave and go out on my own!"

I certainly do! I bit my tongue to keep my thoughts from flying out of my mouth. I gave her a hug and tried to console her. "I know you don't think so right now, but someday, you'll *want* to be out on your own. You'll have big dreams and plans, and you'll be excited to launch. It's my job to make sure you're ready."

She nodded and dried her tears.

"And you'll want to have clean clothes when you chase your dreams, right? You won't be able to buy endless wardrobes—you'll be a broke college student."

> Had I done enough? I'd soon find out.

We both laughed. But I wasn't laughing when she filled her suitcase full of clean clothes to move to college a few years later. By then, she had no qualms about her independence. Partial credit, I suppose, goes toward my hard work in preparing her for the big, bad world she'd encounter. Had I done enough? I'd soon find out. At least she'd have clean clothes, I mused.

The problem was that I'd done everything to equip her and nothing to prepare me for my new lifestyle as an empty nester.

Ready or Not

Within a few years, Mariah and her little sister Katie had found their wings and thrived on their own. Their ability to support themselves and pursue God's calling made me proud, but after pouring my whole identity into being a mom, I didn't know who I was anymore.

What was my purpose, if not a mom? I told everyone that we were happy empty nesters. But deep down, I suspected this phase of life wouldn't ever be 100 percent happy.

I had no local friends who'd launched their kids. All my in-town friends were still in the thick of parenting, so I didn't talk about the negatives; I just focused on the freedom.

One day, while out walking my Boston terrier, I passed a man who shook his head and laughed. Not a "that's so cute" or "how funny" kind of laugh, but a "lady, you are ridiculous" kind of laugh. That's when I realized that my dog's argyle sweater was a little over the top for most people. But in my defense, he did need something to keep warm.

I wonder what the man would have thought had he known that the other outfits in my dog's wardrobe rotation consisted of one red raincoat (with a hood, of course), a waffle costume from the previous Halloween, and a plaid shirt, all of which I kept clean and wrinkle-free. But maybe the random critic in my neighborhood had a point—I couldn't spend the rest of my life with nothing to do but dress my geriatric pet.

> I couldn't spend the rest of my life with nothing to do but dress my geriatric pet.

It's not that I missed the days of clothes piled on the floor next to the laundry hamper or finding my dryer coated in glitter. If I never again had to hoist myself onto the washer to reattach a hose, I wouldn't feel like I'd missed out. But still, I had too much time and too few pair of socks that needed matching.

I asked my husband if I should get a real job, and he looked at me as if I were insane. "You don't like to be told what to do," he said. "And you hate technology. Where would you even work?"

Fair enough. He was right on all points. However, I did have all sorts of time to learn computer skills. And a lot less laundry, argyle dog sweaters notwithstanding. So I worked on the one thing I love to do most: write.

Birthing Pains

I spent my days learning new technology and networking. I'd had a few stories and articles published, but now I looked for freelance assignments full-time. I worked for local and national publications, and my work was even accepted into a few anthologies.

But the big dream was to write a book. I didn't know if I had it in me, but I did have a story that I wanted to tell. My story. Often people would hear about the circumstances from my childhood and wonder aloud how I'd turned out so well. My short answer, "God redeemed me," was about to get a whole lot longer.

> I didn't know if I had it in me, but I did have a story that I wanted to tell.

At a writer's conference, I asked my coach, "Do you think this story could make a whole book?"

"Yes," she said. "I think it's time."

I set a goal to finish the first draft during NaNoWriMo (short for National Novel Writing Month), in which writers around the globe band together in the month of November to put 50,000 words or more on paper. At the end, I had a tattered, stringy mess that resembled a series of journal entries.

After six more drafts, my writing coach finally deemed it good enough to shop to publishers. In the meantime, I entered the first few chapters into a contest for unpublished works.

On awards night, my stomach fluttered when the emcee announced the nonfiction category.

"And the third-place winner is—"

But she didn't call my name.

"In second place—" The emcee paused for effect but again called someone else's name.

Well, then. "That's okay," I whispered to my husband. I squeezed his hand as my heart plummeted. There would be other contests, other opportunities.

"And the first-place winner is—" Again, the nerve-racking pause. "*Curtain Call* by Lyneta Smith."

I looked at my husband. Felt my jaw drop. "What?"

My husband jumped up and applauded. "Whoo!" Around the huge auditorium, other cheers and applause filled the room. I floated to the front and up the stairs, onstage as if in a dream. Finally, validation for all my hard work. Maybe I could, after all, be a real writer.

After networking with dozens of agents and editors, I finally contracted with a small publisher and launched my first "book baby" out into the world.

Launching

My memoir won several awards after publication, and I continued to learn more about the craft of writing. I enrolled in Berkeley's professional editor certificate program. Now I teach other writers how to revise and launch their own book babies.

As with our human babies, we authors make mistakes. We dread letting our precious bundles of joy go. Uncertainty and doubt ride along on every launch. But one thing remains clear: authors with messages of God's love and goodness burning in their hearts can't help anyone else unless their books are crafted with excellence and sent out into the world. I had found my next calling.

As I type this, a clean pile of laundry I dumped on my bed waits for me upstairs. Another hamper full of dirty clothes sits by the washer. I have another load I dried a few days ago tumbling on the wrinkle-release setting, in hopes that I can finally hang up slacks and blouses that won't need ironing.

It reminds me of the good ol' days, but now I'm launching books instead of young adults into the world. I pray that my daughters and the books I help create will impact generations to come.

Empty Nest Barbie

MICHELLE RAYBURN

MY HUSBAND ONCE SAID IF someone were to create a collectible Barbie in my honor, she would be called Don't Touch Me Barbie. This sounded like a Gold Label model for sure. Right up there with Pink Splendor Barbie and Luncheon Ensemble Barbie.

Don't Touch Me Barbie comes with her patented "personal space bubble" feature, equipped with extendable arms that keep unwanted hugs and handshakes at bay. Or a Starbucks cup for one hand and a phone for the other because "My hands are full. Oops! Can't shake today." Her catchphrase? "I'm sorry, but I need my space." She's the perfect companion for those times when you just want to be left alone to binge-watch your favorite show or dive into a good book.

> Some people might say I didn't know what
> I wanted to be when I grew up.

As I wrote a piece about this for my Substack,[6] I realized just how many versions of Barbie I have been in my lifetime. Some people might say I didn't know what I wanted to be when I grew up. I like to think of it as making my plans and then realizing God had other ones. Over. And. Over.

> I like to think of it as making my plans and then realizing God had other ones. Over. And. Over.

Change of Plans

At age twenty-one, I graduated with my Bachelor of Science in nursing, and Optimistic Career Nurse Barbie was born. She came with a clipboard, thermometer, and a blood pressure cuff for interactive play. Her friendly, caring expression was bright, and her attentive and compassionate eyes embodied the passionate dedication of a nursing professional. She may have been dressed in all white, but a touch of pink on her stethoscope and shoes showcased her personality to the world.

Optimistic Career Nurse Barbie also happened to have a teeny-tiny diamond chip and wedding band on her left hand and came with the cutest little cocker spaniel puppy with a pink leash—her attempt at staving off the baby fever. Alas, before much time passed at all, she became Pregnant Puffy Barbie, who squeezed into the uniform and worked the night shift until the week before giving birth.

Optimistic Career Nurse Barbie's optimism faded a bit somewhere in the last trimester, and she second-guessed the puppy and the career. By the time she was Pregnant Puffy Barbie 2.0, she completely released that career, surprising even herself with the newfound desire to be a stay-at-home mom (SAHM).

SAHM Barbie came dressed in a cozy yet comfortable ensemble with pink Crocs and all the essentials for managing a household and caring for her family. Her ponytail could be transformed into a messy bun with the included clip. A tiny bottle of dry shampoo was her best friend. She carried a diaper bag stocked with the essentials that could convert to an on-the-go backpack as her family grew. SAHM Barbie found joy in tending her garden or baking bread, and she had a little clip-on reading light for devouring books late into the night while Ken snored next to her.

Change of Roles

As Barbie's boys grew, she took on the roles of Sporty Mom Barbie, who came with a team jersey with RAYBURN on the back, comfortable jeans, and a signature pink water bottle for baseball games and track meets. She carried a tote filled with snacks and sunscreen, plus a camera to capture everything for the scrapbooks. She had a dual role as Band and Choir Mom Barbie, who lugged around a messenger bag full of sheet music to accompany the choir and soloists at school concerts. Her ensemble included a pink metronome for keeping time and a bonus binder to corral all the choral music. Coral pink, of course.

> As she began to explore, she tucked a few skills into her collection and added accessories.

In the midst of the years of being all the Barbies, this mom started to look ahead to the day when she would be none of these things. Should she go back to being Optimistic Career Nurse Barbie? Did she want to? As she began to explore, she tucked a few skills into her collection and added accessories. A pink laptop to explore writing. And Bible tools for speaking and teaching. She attended some conferences for writing and speaking and added brightly colored sweaters and business casual slacks and shoes to her collection. She polished her skills, polished her nails, and spread the word that Piano Teacher Barbie was also available part-time.

SAHM Sporty Music Writer Speaker Mom Barbie had a lot of sorting to do. It was hard to do all the things and still find time to read books anymore. Barbie fell into bed exhausted every night as she juggled all the roles. She even had a three-year stint amid everything else as Glutton for Punishment Barbie, where she completed a graduate degree.

And then came the day she had seen on the horizon for a while.

Change of Life

As SAHM Barbie and all her alter egos cruised into perimenopause, her boys began cruising out on their own. College wasn't exactly an empty nest, but within two years, Barbie had no more trombones tooting and practicing up the hall. No more piano plunking or guitar strumming. Goodbye, band and choir. So long, baseball games and track meets. Adios mega-baking and meal prepping. Hello, cheater glasses and memory lapses.

SAHM Barbie became Exploring Her Options Barbie as she tried a new career. She wore chic, yet relaxed and flowy outfits to the office with soft sweaters to navigate fluctuating body temperatures and menstrual nightmares. Maxi skirts galore. Her pink Jeep—actually, a red Cherokee, more practical than the Wrangler—put on the miles as Barbie commuted to the city every day. Ken tinkered in the garage at night on his classic Jeeps while Barbie collapsed in exhaustion on the Dream in Pink chaise lounge inside the Barbie DreamHouse.

And then, the boys got married. Barbie drifted into menopause with unexpected ease. *Thank you, Lord, for that grace,* she prayed each time a bestie had a hot flash. Ken drifted to sleep earlier and earlier. Barbie traded her commute for freelance work from her home office. *I can be whatever I want to be,* she thought. The doors opened for more writing and ministry opportunities.

Change of Pace

Enter Empty Nest Barbie. She's a work in progress who exudes a sense of freedom and adventure. Her middle section is fluffier, and her clothing ultra-comfortable. "Skinny jeans be gone" is her motto. This Barbie comes with a smallish purse with enough room for a smartphone to keep in touch with her grown-up kids. The days of carrying bags bigger than a suitcase to haul everyone else's junk are long past.

Empty Nest Barbie exchanged her long, flowing hair for a feisty, stylish blonde bob, and she comes with tweezers for plucking the rogue chin hairs and unruly eyebrows. Plus those cheater glasses.

Whether she's planning an adventure, redecorating her home, or volunteering in her community, Empty Nest Barbie is a testament to the joy and fulfillment that comes with this new phase of life. She prioritizes self-care, and the set includes a little pink hammock for reading and sipping iced coffee in her downtime.

Empty Nest Barbie works hard, but she knows the value of quiet and serene sabbath rest too. She encourages the celebration of life's transitions, reminding everyone that there are always new opportunities to grow and explore. She started a podcast and likes to blog. Now, she still attends baseball games sometimes, but as the mom of the coach rather than a student. She takes vacations with Ken and enjoys wooded hikes and walks on rugged Great Lakes beaches.

> At the heart of every phase, this gal knows that her identity and worth come from God.

At the heart of every phase, this gal knows that her identity and worth come from God. And he's sure surprised her along the way with each blessing and challenge. Part of her identity has been being a mom. But so much of who she is centers around the unique gifts and abilities God placed in her at birth. As she sees her children use their own gifts and abilities, she embraces change with grace and resilience. Launch phase and parenting duties completed, she knows that her role in this new chapter is one of support, encouragement, and inspiration.

As Empty Nest Barbie serves as a role model to her children, she demonstrates the importance of resilience, adaptability, and self-discovery. The unbreakable family ties only grow stronger as she aspires to provide a safe and non-judgmental space for her adult children to express themselves, share their struggles, and celebrate their successes. She can offer a listening ear, words of wisdom, and practical advice. Whether or not she is Barbie, she will always be Mom.

Doing the Next Thing

SUE DONALDSON

Y LIFE CHANGED FOREVER THE day our firstborn daughter arrived—
on time, mind you—followed by two more (all girls) in the
ensuing seven years. It's difficult to remember my life before
that auspicious date: November 18, 1988. No one prepares you for
that heart-filled and throat-clogged moment. Nor for the years and
years of moments that follow.

Clamor and Commotion

I just did what most moms do, which was to do the next thing:
changed diapers, made playdates, hosted soccer team parties, coached
on how to interview for a first job, and listened to dating disasters
and heartbreaks. Later, I scooped up boxes and luggage full of new
towels and the latest sneakers, plus great hopes and dreams—ready
for college. A few more years, and it was setting up first apartments. I
experienced all of these moments times three.

Life was full for years. Then, one day, I made brownies, and there
was no one to save the spatula for, so I had to lick the bowl all by
myself.

Having not had children until age thirty-six (and not stopping
until forty-three), I'd been too busy (and tired) to think about empty

nesting. On wonderful days with cooperative, sunny children, it seemed deadly; on normal days, it seemed far away; on hard days, it seemed fantasy-like. Being mostly self-contained and able to do things by myself—thank you very much—I didn't worry about its imminent arrival.

And then, boom. Our youngest, Mary, graduated from high school early on a Thursday and left for Iowa on Sunday to stay with my husband Mark's great family for the next three months. Boom. Again.

Someone warned me that would happen. I didn't mind the empty nest early on. With the clamor and drama of the endings and goings, I needed the quiet. And I began filling any space with people I'd had to put off for various reasons those last few months.

> Even when I didn't see it happening, God had been preparing me for this big change in a most gracious way.

Even when I didn't see it happening, God had been preparing me for this big change in a most gracious way. Since the girls were little, we'd rented an extra room to international students, sometimes two, as extra rooms became available. After our girls flew the coop, I'd get asked, "So, how's the empty nesting going?"

I'd smile and reply, "We just said *adios* to two girls from Spain this week but look forward to a young man from China arriving next week. It's not exactly empty."

But eventually, we even stopped that season of hosting and caring for other people's children. Forty or more international students later, it was time.

Projects and People

There are days I wish Mom were around so I could ask her, "How did you and Dad rearrange your lives when all five of us Moore kids finally launched?" Maybe that's why Dad bought a Lindal Cedar Home in his late sixties. A Lindal Cedar Home is like LEGO blocks for adults. All the pieces arrive, including every last nail and diagram. Dad hadn't retired yet, but with Mom's help, he spent the next five years, every vacation time, building their second home in Paradise (not the real Paradise—the town Paradise in Northern California.)

On any given day or conversation, Dad, whipping out photos of their latest accomplishment from his front pocket, became an evangelist for building your own home in your sixties. We'd tease him and say, "Dad, most men your age show off pictures of their grandchildren, but we get to revel in the latest area you've cleared for a half-basement."

He'd chuckle and say, "Did I show you what we did last week?"

We delighted in their delight. They filled their empty nest with a beautiful project they worked on together in a new town with a new church family. As my husband—whom I affectionately call the Man in Plaid—and I faced our next season, I asked the Lord, "What could Mark and I do together that would foster delight in creativity and a closer relationship with one another?" I could add to that prayer, "And would keep us out of our adult kids' hair!"

We don't know the complete answer to that question yet, but I look for smaller ways than building a whole house in another part of the state to bring us together—we're still not finished with the remodel on *this* one. But we are drawn together by things like hosting our former international students and their parents when they come to town. Or co-leading our bi-monthly Growth Group or planning trips for just two instead of five.

My mentor told me years ago, "Sue, any time you invest in people or the Word is a worthy occupation because both last forever."

Investing in our marriage is part of that worthy occupation, one that might have been placed on a shelf for a short season. It was time to reach for it again and place it front and center, to learn again why we married each other and why we still loved each other. Each of us has changed, and in good ways. We have the time now to appreciate those changes.

> Investing in our marriage is part of that worthy occupation.

Another thing we observed from our folks was that Mom and Dad knew how to make friends. I know they loved us best and most, but friends and more friends filled their hearts and homes. Mom used to say with utmost seriousness, "Your dad and I have to keep making new, younger friends because our friends keep dying." True to their word, they were surrounded by dear folks of all ages when they finally went to glory in their mid-nineties.

Friends and Fun

If some of your kids are still underfoot, keep cultivating those friendships that last beyond diapers and soccer and proms. Make your own playdates now. God will surprise you when you least expect it. When our eldest was in kindergarten, we hosted our first birthday party for Jesus and invited her whole class. The morning of the event, the mother of one of her classmates called to ask, "Will you be reading from the Bible at this party?"

We didn't know one another, and I was a little startled by her question, but I replied, "We will be reading the Christmas story based in the Bible. Would you like to come and help with the crafts?"

She came and returned for the next ten years of birthday parties for Jesus. We stayed good friends, even after our daughters went their separate ways. We had coffee just the other day and encouraged each other in our faith.

When I keep my antennae up for people who need to be in

my life and at my table—for their sake and mine—there's rarely an empty seat or couch. And I'm grateful. Last night, two college seniors came for dinner and shared their heart needs and plans for their next steps. I gave them chicken and rice and coffee ice cream and sent them home with their own loaf of banana bread, and all were blessed.

Last Tuesday, sixteen women filled the front room for dessert and a chance to make a new friend—three from my gym, a couple from work, some from church. Most didn't know each other, and several were not of faith that I could tell, but with a couple of non-intrusive but intriguing conversation starters, we experienced community and perhaps dissipated some feeling of loneliness in a small but glorious way. Part of filling my empty nest is helping another feel less isolated, and in so doing, I'm filled as well.

The Next Thing

I learned early on that my husband, Mark, was not to be my end-all for living a complete and satisfied life. He's only human, after all. And it's the same with my kids. They filled my life 24/7 for many years, but they aren't the most important part of my life. Nor is my career role or ministry. God is my end-all, to the best of my ability, which usually means, as far as I surrender each day to him.

> I learned early on that my husband was not to be my end-all for living a complete and satisfied life.

I read Colossians 3:11 this morning: "Christ is all and in all." I believe it and try to live it, but I still cry when the girls leave after a short visit. It's just the way it is. I can't help it. I tell Mark we need to watch an action movie and order take-out because I will be crying in about twenty minutes when Bonnie (or Bethany or Mary) leaves. As long as it's Mexican food, he's in.

No matter what stage I'm in, there's always a "What's next?" around the bend. It's a great way to live once I get over the shock that, once again, my days and my months will look different than they have looked before.

> Five years ago, I started a podcast. I didn't even know what a podcast was.

Five years ago, I started a podcast. I didn't even know what a podcast was. But my all-in-all God made all the pieces fall together, and it not only fills an empty nest, but my kids are also proud of me—a lovely bonus. I might text the family thread, "Please don't call me because I'm recording for an hour." And they will patiently remind me that I have the capacity to silence my notifications or some such thing. I just smile and remember I taught them how to tie their shoes and set a proper table.

Whenever I strike an I-wonder-what's-next pose, I like to ask my mentor of twenty-five years what God's will is for my life. Laurie doesn't take the bait. She smiles sweetly and says, "Trust God, and do the next thing." She wants me to obey God, not her. Annoying at times. But she's right, and it works. I just need to listen.

Of course, David said it first:

> Trust in the Lord and do good.
> Then you will live safely in the land and prosper.
> Take delight in the Lord,
> and he will give you your heart's desires.
> Commit everything you do to the Lord.
> Trust him, and he will help you. (Psalm 37:3–5)

One thing about an empty nest is that I have more time to slow down and stop and listen to God. Do I do it? Sometimes. And when I do, he fills my nest with good things.

> I have more time to slow down and stop and listen to God. Do I do it? Sometimes.

Mark and I might sit at times and stare and not say much other than, "Did you hear from Mary (Bonnie) (Bethany) today?" Hearing from those chicks remains the highlight of our days. These same chicks remind the Man in Plaid on occasion that FaceTiming every day is not exactly necessary. *Just wait until they have chicks*, I muse.

How many times have I said that? Thought that? Too many to count. It's a waste of time.

What's not a waste of time is coming alongside others who may need what Mark and I have learned from life and God—or from making mistakes—and going forward no matter what. What's not a waste of time is inviting people to my table and couches and baking in advance to have loaves and fishes ready to share. What's not a waste of time is telling God each morning, "I'm yours, Lord. I surrender all. You are my end-all, and I trust you. Show me what you want me to do today (And I still miss my kids. I know you understand that, Lord.) Thank you, and amen."

Contagious Role Models

LORI VOBER

WE ALL START OUR PARENTING journey in different ways. Some of us had our kids through traditional pregnancies. Others became parents through foster care, adoption, or by marriage. No matter how the journey began, I believe most parents start out with similar expectations and dreams for their children, and ultimately, we want our kids to feel loved and supported yet be independent, successful adults.

Parenting 101

When I was a teenager, I was in the generation that went through driver's ed classes at school before getting my license. There were instructions before getting behind the wheel. No matter how you become a parent, sadly, there is very little training involved ahead of time, and most of our training becomes on-the-job learning!

I was that woman who dreamed of what it would be like to be pregnant and could not wait to start our family. I had designed the nursery in my mind, planned how I would tell my spouse I was pregnant, and made a future work strategy and savings plan to live the lifestyle we wanted to and still stay home with our child. There was only one small problem with my thought-out plans. Month after month, I was not getting pregnant. I don't believe my husband had any idea how much starting a family meant to me, and I didn't fully recognize my own struggles at the time.

Rarely Like We Expected

In January 2003, I made the decision to transition my career from corporate marketing and sales in the airline industry to the office manager position at our church. I thought my lack of getting pregnant was related to stress, travel, and schedule, so a change in job would be a good answer. I have a strong faith and will always be thankful for that job change, but God did not provide that new job for a family planning opportunity but to ultimately save my life. Three weeks into my new job, I suffered a massive hemorrhagic stroke that left me paralyzed on the left side.

My husband, Dainis, and I quickly learned that life could change in an instant, and life started all over again with relearning how to sit up straight, stand, and eventually walk. At the point of hospital discharge, we were just celebrating our fifth wedding anniversary. We had honeymooned in the Bahamas, and traveled to Jamaica, Cancun, and Europe. We knew what it meant to celebrate our wins together and stand together in our losses. Our wedding vows were more than words; they were words put into action.

> We knew what it meant to celebrate our wins together and stand together in our losses.

I spent two months in the hospital recovering from the stroke and left the hospital in a wheelchair. Two months after my hospital discharge, Dainis lost his job at Northwest Airlines due to the slowdown in the airline industry after the terrorist attacks of September 11. We moved to Arizona for his new job, and my therapy and recovery continued. I concentrated on therapy for many years after my stroke and treated it like my full-time job. We decided in 2010 that we would again like to consider starting a family. Because of my disability and epilepsy from the stroke, we chose to embrace adoption. In April 2012, we adopted a sibling group of three from Colombia, South America. Our kids were ages six, eight, and ten at the time of adoption—a son and two daughters.

I don't know what we expected when we adopted. We read books and went through adoption training. We heard love doesn't solve all problems, but we really didn't understand. We fell in love with our kids' pictures long before we met them, like a parent falls in love with their baby's ultrasound. We so desperately wanted to be parents and had waited so long for this reality to happen.

> We so desperately wanted to be parents and had waited so long for this reality to happen.

We didn't understand abandonment, trauma, rejection, multiple displacements, and how much that had affected our kids and ultimately would affect our family. It was not like giving birth to triplets, where the board was a clean slate for us to fill up with good, wholesome lessons. It was like getting triplets that were opinionated, vocal, scared and against change, and so hurt.

Dainis and I will both be forever grateful that we had the opportunity to be parents and thankful that our kids' adoption provided that opportunity for us. There were blessings with the challenges, and I don't believe God is finished writing our story yet.

By adopting our kids and giving them the love and support they needed to start thriving in this world, they have gone on to leave a legacy beyond just us. Had we never adopted them, that may or may not have happened. Both of our daughters now have children, so that is one more generation that has bloomed from our love.

From Parenting to Empty Nesting

No matter how you start your parenting journey and at what age your kids are when they come into your life, I believe those are some of the hardest years on you as a person and your marriage as a couple. There is always something and someone to juggle, and kids are, by nature, selfish. Then you usually add pets, activities, chores and responsibilities, a job, and life can be a circus during those first twenty years!

> Here you are, full circle again, just you and your spouse.

Before you know it, the kids graduate and leave home either for work or school, and here you are, full circle again, just you and your spouse. But so much has changed since the last time you were alone, and for many couples, this is where the reality of empty nesting sometimes gets even tougher than the circus of parenting. Couples go from chaos to quiet overnight.

As hard as our journey with our kids was, I almost have to say thank you to them now for the blessing they gave us of both parenting and empty nesting. Before becoming parents, Dainis and I did not have the typical marriage and one that my heart desired for us. He had a great job, we had a great lifestyle, and he loved me very much. But he worked second shift, odd days off as an aircraft mechanic, and I worked normal business hours. So our time was limited, and communication was not typical of most young couples. We did not eat dinner or take walks around the block every night together in our first years of marriage.

After my stroke and his job loss, nothing was normal as he became more of my caregiver. Just as I started getting better, he established a "normal" business career, and life reflected some sense of normalcy. Then, we adopted three kids. So our current new empty nest stage is almost like a new beginning. We love each other the same yet differently because we have walked such an amazingly hard road together, filled with both medical and parenting challenges.

I have learned many things through the years, and in many ways, my husband is my best friend and knows me better than anyone else. However, men and women are made very differently, and many times, he does not have the capacity to take on everything that I want to share. So it's important for women to have women friends to talk to, guys to have guy friends and their own hobbies, and then you have things you love to do together.

My husband loves nature and taking long walks. We just purchased a second home a few hours from our current home that will be a future retirement spot. It is near a lake and walking trails, and it reminds him of Minnesota, where he grew up. Communication and patience are key in any relationship, and if we are clear with each other on our expectations, everything works well.

> Our job was to raise them to the best of our ability and equip them to be the most responsible independent adults they can be.

As women, we often carry a lot of mom guilt for our kids, especially if they leave our home and are not thriving. We have to realize our kids were with us for a short time, and our job was to raise them to the best of our ability and equip them to be the most responsible independent adults they can be to flourish in this world.

Whether our kids listen to us, follow our direction, are successful, or happy is out of our control. We can continue to love, support, and pray for them with healthy boundaries, but our focus needs to be on our own health, our relationship with God, and the needs of our spouse after they leave our nest.

Next Steps

As empty nesters, if we concentrate on leaving the best legacy we can, serving our God as best we can, and living our own best life, our actions and attitude can be a contagious role model for others around us, including our children. We all want our family to be thriving, happy, and healthy, but we ultimately only have control over ourselves.

I realized when my oldest daughter left home right after high school, and we were in the middle of the pandemic, God had given me a unique story to tell as a young stroke survivor and adoptive mom, and sharing my experiences could help others. My journey of sharing was a slow one while my two younger children were still finishing high school, but I have continued my efforts to use my journey to help others. A couple of years ago, I published my first book and then attended my first speaker's conference.

Sharing my story with others, including the lessons my experiences taught me, has served so many purposes. It has given me an opportunity to connect with others who have had similar circumstances. It has taught me the value of reflection and given me the opportunity to cope and heal with some of my own losses. It has given me a chance to encourage others. It has helped me use my challenges and disability for a purpose. It has given my adult children a role model as I strive to serve God as we are called.

We often cannot change what we go through, and we will all be impacted by unexpected challenges and hard trials during our lifetime. We can choose our reaction to our circumstances, and as empty nesters, we are now free to take a lifetime of experiences and make a difference in someone else's life, one person at a time.

Color My Nest Empty

BETH BARRON

DROVE BY THE HIGH SCHOOL a couple of times a week on the way to the grocery store, but during my youngest son's senior year, I felt pangs of premature nostalgia. The red brick building held many men, women, and students who had invested in my son's life.

How many times will I enter that building again, I wondered. *At how many more track meets will I cheer and navigate the social scene of track parents and drama mamas?* How many more plays would I enjoy? And the more practical consideration: how would we get all the chores done at home without my son's help?

The dynamics of our home would change. My husband and I would have more time alone.

As my son's friends tromped up and down our basement stairs, I wondered, *How many more evenings will be filled with loud teenagers playing Nintendo and scavenging in the pantry?*

Multicolored or Monochrome

As graduation approached, I tried to avoid helicopter mama role. (Don't ask my son how well I did.) Instead, I savored each day of boys in the backyard grilling their own hamburgers. A day of teenage berry picking led to a bunch of boys commandeering my kitchen to make pies and exclaiming later to themselves, "This is the best pie I've ever eaten."

I feared the Technicolor days of a noisy, full house would turn to boring black and white. I expected the quiet to drown me.

Soon enough, at the end of the summer, young men scattered to their various universities. My youngest loaded his car and took off to his dream school with enthusiasm. I wondered if his dream would be my nightmare.

I expected to feel sad. After a teary-eyed final prayer and good-bye, I didn't.

I expected to feel weepy each time I passed the high school on the way to buy groceries. However, I hardly noticed it as I drove by.

> Despite my earlier efforts to be hands-off, I piloted that helicopter of motherhood a bit too enthusiastically.

What I didn't expect was what I did feel—an incredible aware-ness of freedom. Despite my earlier efforts to be hands-off, I piloted that helicopter of motherhood a bit too enthusiastically. So, when I let go of the controls, the weight of hands-on motherhood disap-peared. In its place I found new opportunities and challenges.

During my son's sophomore year of college, we relocated to another state and city—that certainly busied my heart and mind. Could God supply treasured friends in our new location? He did.

I continued working part-time but asked to add some hours to my work schedule to better serve my workplace. Dismayed that I did not get to work more hours, I began to explore other options. I was shocked to discover I was qualified to teach English to new immigrants at a nearby community college—so the job description said anyway.

Do they really think I can do this? I'm not sure I can.

Variegated Changes

First, I had to become a learner. I hadn't written a resume in years, so my older sons—long out of the nest—made suggestions and proofread my writing. Eventually, I went to my first job interview in years. I was thrilled and shocked that I got the job and signed a contract.

That was the easy part.

Now I had to master new skills. As I started teaching one course and then two, the learning curve took my breath away.

Years before when I taught art to middle school students, I wrote assignments on the board and my grades in a pale green grade book. Now I had to learn to set up an online page and update it regularly. I taught using a smart board and entered grades online.

With each new challenge, I took a deep breath and said to myself, "Plunge in." Colleagues, often younger ones, helped along the way. Eventually, I found a rhythm to teaching and found my niche at a nearby non-profit, serving refugees.

My husband and I also worked with international students along with others from our church. We welcomed large groups of students from a nearby university into our home. I learned how to make fragrant *dal* for twenty, using unfamiliar spices and slicing the onions up and down into long strips the way one student's mother does. Our home was again filled with rowdy laughter as we played Pit with a group of Indian students.

I also decided to attend a nearby seminary. *Does my university even have my transcript anymore? Who do I ask to write references?* I wondered.

This brought the joy of attending graduate classes. At orientation, I felt conspicuously unfashionable as trim young women in strappy sandals listened intently to the speakers. Their stylish hair and clothes made me long for a makeover. And was that gray hair sprouting from my scalp? Yes, and a spindly gray one on my chin as well.

I felt out of place but was welcomed by my classmates and professors. My classmates helped me understand online assignments, and I pushed a classmate's baby in a stroller in the back of the classroom. I learned new skills I excelled in and others I was not so proficient at.

Wading through pages of reading stretched me. But besides biblical education, I studied writing. We, students, helped each other write better and developed a respect for one another's gifts.

I joined a group of talented Christian bloggers and had the thrill and satisfaction of publishing some articles and even a poem for other publications.

> I found my life overflowing with new demands and unexpected opportunities.

Once worried that my Technicolor world would become black and white, I found my life overflowing with new demands and unexpected opportunities. I reveled in colorful scarves, countless languages, Ethiopian coffee, and syrupy nut-filled pastries in the morning and a demanding seminary class in the afternoons.

Kaleidoscopic Joy

These days, my refugee students and I explore the challenges of the English language, giggling together as they comprehend the difference between "I cooked my family" and "I cooked for my family." I teach them things I'd never thought about before, such as the proper order for adjectives. I pointed out the difference between "uncle" and "ankle"—words that sounded identical to them.

Did I summit every mountain successfully in all these new endeavors? Definitely not.

I deeply hurt the feelings of an older student in my English class, but in time, this older gentleman and I learned to give and receive appreciation. Knowing this man has given me wisdom in relating to other students who were prominent in their own cultures and now must struggle to read and write with the competency of elementary students. They now have my highest regard.

I applied for a writing position focused on refugees and immigrants. And I got turned down. But in the end, my empty nest brims with joy, opportunity, and a lot of hard work.

> My empty nest brims with joy, opportunity, and a lot of hard work.

I've navigated new transitions and let go of new blessings. My sons are all well-established adults, two with families of their own. I've treasured every moment with my grandchildren, and now I'm releasing one family of children and grandchildren to live abroad, trusting that God can care for them better than I ever can. They will be shaped and stretched by the challenges of their lives.

As I write this, I'm looking at yet another change of my own. After much thought and prayer, my husband and I plan to take a step back from our current jobs and transition to ministry in retirement. He wants to relocate to another city. I'm sorting through years of accumulation, packing, and trying not to panic.

Years of following God and trusting him don't dull my emotions as I say farewell to dear friends and, at times, fellow mischief-makers. I look ahead, wondering if my world, now filled with friends, a great church, and a kaleidoscope of students from many nations, will turn black and white.

But then I look back at God's faithfulness in my empty nest, and I have hope amid change that my world will again be filled with color.

Rescue Me!

DEBORAH DEARMOND

HAVEN'T HAD A REAL JOB in years. At least, that's what my kids used to say. You know, a real job, in an office building, with other people and maybe an elevator. Or, at the very least, a break room with a refrigerator full of "science projects" underway from colleagues who decided that fast-food chicken strips and fries sounded better than last night's tuna casserole they bagged and brought with every good intention.[7]

> If you turn around and there's nobody behind you moving in the same direction, you are not leading.

Oh, I've worked. And I would say that I *do* have a real job—more accurately, a business. I am a professional coach and consultant. For the past twenty-four years, I've officed at home and commuted—usually on an airplane—to various clients in a broad range of industries. My specialty? Leadership training, development, and coaching. Helping people develop the skills to lead, not just manage, others. I don't care what your title is; if you turn around and there's nobody behind you moving in the same direction, you are not leading. Fortunately for me, the world is full of managers and bosses, but leaders are in short supply these days.

Time for a Change

Over the last two and a half years, I've been blessed to work with one of the nation's most powerful players in the transportation business. I've been workin' on the railroad. (It's hard not to sing as I type it!) A rich 150-plus years of heritage and history, and much of it has remained unchanged in attitudes, mindset, and management methodology.

But the last several years or so have brought a new realization: the "way we've always done it" won't work anymore. It's time to make a change and begin creating an entirely different culture by developing leaders who can take them there.

It's a slow and steady process. So many come into the classroom quite wary, almost suspicious. "Is this gonna be a 'hold hands and sing Kum Ba Yah' kinda thing?" one big burly guy in overalls asked me, definitely out of his comfort zone.

"Nope," I replied. "We're going to give you some tools for communicating well and dealing successfully with conflict on the job. No fluffy stuff," I assured him. That was almost true.

Perceived Value

One of our activities is titled The Rescue Mission. The format is simple: the group must come to a consensus as to which five of the ten stranded occupants they will rescue as a devastating storm closes in on a tiny remote island. The five who remain will be washed out to sea and will not survive.

Participants are asked to select from the list of individuals with only a very brief description of each. They are instructed first to make their individual choices, and then they must discuss the possibilities and come to a consensus as a group. No voting is allowed, and they are reminded to use their newly acquired communication skills to achieve their decision. *It's a little fluffy.* They have twenty-five minutes in total.

Here's the challenge: the info provided about each of the island occupants is designed to encourage the participants to base their selections on their *personal values.*

Some guys go with the *women and children.* Some select those they believe have the *greatest value to society.* Others take the *youngest,* as they have their whole lives ahead of them. Some ignore the impending storm's reality altogether and select those they believe are *strong enough to survive* on the island.

When we discuss our values, we can get pretty passionate when challenged by others; it creates a great platform for using the skills they've learned. I've seen the discussions get heated, and people get offended. I've seen them end up in a stalemate, unable to successfully come to a decision. And I've seen it work beautifully, with the new skills taking a starring role in building understanding, influence, and collaboration. Whichever way it goes, the learning is rich.

> The occupant described as a "fifty-five-year-old housewife with a high school education" is gonna die.

Here is another interesting response I've observed from watching this discussion unfold. The occupant described as a "fifty-five-year-old housewife with a high school education" is gonna die.

She's Not Finished!

She occasionally makes someone's initial "keep" list, but she rarely gets on that rescue chopper. Even those in favor of *women and children* are typically easily persuaded to leave her behind. I have done this activity roughly twice a week for the last three months, and it's consistent across the board: she's a floater. Why? Here's how the conversation goes:

"Man, she's fifty-five! Come on, she's lived her life already."

"How many more old housewives does this world need?"

"She doesn't have any kids at home. They're all raised up. She's done her job."

"What's she got left on her plate? Die; that's the only thing left."

Ouch. That's me. I am older than fifty-five. Heck, I'm over sixty-five. My kids are grown and raising families of their own.

But I am nowhere near ready to say I have lived all the life God has for me. Many of the things he placed on my plate, I have indeed completed. But there are many items left on my to-do list. So, I may be done, but I'm not finished!

> **I may be done, but I'm not finished!**

I must admit I am incensed, indignant, and infuriated each time I hear this discussion. But if it's such a consistently common perspective, I believe there is probably a bigger image problem than I might have ever understood.

It's not that those of us who are fifty-plus are no longer capable, qualified, or called. It's that lots of us believe the lie that we have nothing left to offer—so we just stopped showing up.

Why? How on earth did that happen?

For some of us, we find it terribly lonely in that empty nest. Braces are paid for, Little League games have concluded, and piano practice has been silenced. We spent so many years focused on discussions with our husbands about the kids that we'd forgotten how to converse about anything else. There's an awkwardness that seems rather isolating. Some of us are alone, indeed; divorce we didn't see coming or widowhood. When you've been part of "we" and "us" for a long time, the transition to "I" can be scary.

Others in our group are less than engaged by the career they pursued and now find it dull and confining. Perhaps we just long to do something new or different, maybe even called to it, but it seems that opportunity has come and gone. "Best to leave that to one of the younger girls." "Short-term humanitarian trip to help in Haiti? Maybe ten years ago, but now? I don't think so."

We flounder as we try to figure out the answer to the question, "OK, Lord, so what's my purpose now?"

Time to Shine

Being needed is a heady drug and unbelievably addictive. Our children needed us for survival, a level of need that was both over-whelming and affirming. Our husbands needed our encouragement and support as they built their careers. PTA needed room mothers, Little League needed a snack lady, and neighbors needed carpool drivers. And they invited us! Certainly, while we were doing it, it drove us crazy, but it reminded us we were of value.

We still need that affirmation of our usefulness, and the good news is that there are many places to get that fix. Now, finally, at this time in our lives, we are available and free to explore our options, and they're a lot more interesting than driving the carpool! This is not the time to drag out the knitting and settle in for the "winter of our lives."

Adventure has no age limit.

Adventure has no age limit. There are new friendships to build and relationships to resurrect. It's never too late to serve, explore, mentor, study, create, or minister. It's time to *shine* during this time of our life. We can make a genuine difference in the lives of others and fully walk in the wisdom and joy we have collected this far on our journey. We are relevant. We have value. We are *not* past tense!

Fed Up and Revved Up

"For everything there is a season, a time for every activity under heaven" (Ecclesiastes 3:1). Each season of our lives has a purpose, but it's a bit of a moving target. As we change, our purpose changes too!

Author Erma Bombeck once said, "When I stand before God at the end of my life, I would hope that I would not have a single bit of talent left but could say I've used everything you gave me."[8] That is my heart's desire. Don't tightly clutch your remaining talent—invest it, share it, and give it away!

An old proverb says, "If you want to go fast, go alone. If you want to go far, go together." I love this concept, and I'm looking for traveling buddies to help me finish strong. So, who's up for adventure? Take a look at relationships, spiritual growth, health and wellness, beauty, confidence, and communication—all focused on where we are right now. We're not forty anymore. Fifty is a beautiful place to plant new hope, new awareness, and crazy good adventures. New times and new opportunities need new ideas and new tools.

Gather your peeps and plan to go far together. Explore the possibilities for those of us who are fed up with the stereotype and revved up enough to ask, "What's my purpose now?"

Celebrating Relationships and Connections

Take Me with You

LISA-ANNE WOOLDRIDGE

The brown packing tape judders across the lips of the box
Sealing inside the shiny trophies, silly ribbons, and game balls,
Once so proudly displayed, the forgotten treasures of a small boy.

I press my own lips together, sealing in the soft words,
The relics of childhood, outgrown names, murmurs and prayers
Often whispered into the curls of a sleeping child in arms.

The joy of embarking is on his face as he prepares to leave,
High spirits and hopes for adventure nestled into milk crates,
Laundry hampers filled with new linens for a strange new bed.

I try to mirror his smile, mine, a little less wide and sure,
As he tosses his favorite, worn-out hiking boots on the pile
Of things he wants to keep, to carry, to hold on to from home.

The sob remains hidden in the back of my throat—old shoes
Seem out of place next to all the new clothes I insisted he have.
But they are broken in, comfortable, with lots of tread yet on
the soles.

When he wears them, I pray, he will remember all the days
We walked together, at first on my hip, then hand-in-hand,
Before he bounded off ahead to become this beautiful man.

Empty Rooms, Full Heart

MICHELLE RAYBURN

FROM THE MOMENT THEY EAT solid food, our kids start leaving. When they can pinch a Cheerio in those chubby little fingers, it's the earliest decipherable hieroglyph on the wall of independence, saying they won't need us someday. Not for spoon-feeding or diapering. Not for baths, or chicken nuggets, or transportation services. Not for goodnight kisses or bedtime stories.

They leave gradually, turning up the heat slowly so as not to scald our hearts with their sudden absence. The first notch is a half day at Grandma's, then at a friend's house. They come home with stories of the fun they had, the cookies baked, the pastures explored, and fishing at the pond. A half day becomes a whole day when friends play paintball or head to the waterpark. One more notch.

Then, an overnight for a friend's birthday party. It becomes a weekend for a class trip. And then it's more and more notches. Long stretches where their bedsheets and comforter aren't tussled and left heaped in disarray—the first indication of how that room might look as a guest room—and the usual pile of dirty laundry doesn't build up on their bedroom floor. There are no ice cream bowls or dirty sweatshirts left on the coffee table. No toothpaste on the counter or toilet seats left up.

A Brief Parting

When my firstborn signed up for a summer mission trip to Bolivia, we did the passport application, saw the travel nurse for immunizations, did the Visa paperwork. Packed and repacked. Discussed scenarios, safety, medications, and first aid. And then, there were fourteen days of silence, except for an email or two from the mission leader with updates.

> These are the dress rehearsals for when they pack up crates of stuff and head off to a dorm room.

These are the dress rehearsals for when they pack up crates of stuff and head off to a dorm room for longer stretches of time away. To halls that smell of chocolate chip cookies baking in the common kitchen, masking the lingering scents of dirty socks and boy smells from semesters gone by—and the very distinct skunky scent of weed somewhere down the maze of hallways and doors.

And then, it's us doing the leaving. Saying goodbye and driving away with an empty trailer to a vacant house. Praying the weed smokers would stay down the hall. Far away. Praying the kids would make smart decisions. Hoping they would miss us just a little.

They returned for holidays and summers—and a semester of student teaching when they were flat broke—but then there was a proposal and a ring, save-the-date cards, and invitations. And while it felt sudden then, they had been leaving for the last twenty-five years.

A Long Farewell

Although it may be tempting to equate this whole process with losing little pieces of our hearts, the empty spots at the table, the perfectly mitered corners on the bed quilt in their still-clean room, and the absence of stinky teenagers in what is now going to become your sewing room are not signs of your empty heart.

This new life is not the chorus of a sad and sappy country song.

> The house feels so big, but my heart feels so small,
> I'm a sad mom with an empty nest, missing it all.

No. The last few decades have had many heart-filling moments. Launching a child into the world is also a process of gradually finding ourselves. The lyric is more like this:

> Little by little, as the kids grow and roam,
> I'm finding myself, rediscovering my own.

Letting go is not just about preparing children for independence—it's also about mothers rediscovering themselves outside of their role as caregivers. Our priorities gradually change. When I brought a newborn home from the hospital, my priority was keeping him alive. And that first week was scary.

Then my priority became teaching him now to pour milk for himself and make a sandwich. Taking responsibility for his decisions and actions. Being kind and polite, becoming a good human. My priority soon changed to helping him manage money, plan for a future.

And while he planned for his future, I was planning for mine. I finished my master's degree while my boys were in middle school. And started thinking about what I would do if I went back to work. Planning ahead for when we might take our first vacation as a couple. Dreaming of what it would be like to have an open calendar.

A New Shift

As our children leave home, we're faced with an opportunity to reevaluate our priorities, pursue long-neglected passions, and invest in our own personal growth and well-being. This transition can be both liberating and daunting as we navigate the shifting dynamics of our relationships and redefine our sense of purpose beyond motherhood.

We can be steadfast and committed to supporting and empowering our children as they spread their wings while also finding joy and fulfillment in our own journeys. We can miss our children without wasting away because of their absence. Feeling excitement about their leaving does not indicate a lack of love or nurturing. It's exciting for them too!

> In all these years of their gradual departure, you have changed.

In all these years of their gradual departure, you have changed. You aren't the same person you were when you brought a squirmy little bundle home from the hospital. Sure, you have wrinkles now and probably some gray hair—I like to say mine is self-highlighting. But this new version of you is pretty cool.

A Settled Contentment

As an older and wiser version of myself, I actually like who I am now. I want to be friends with her. She has found her voice and knows what she wants. We've weathered sarcasm like a champ. Learned to speak it fluently and interpret glances, rolled eyes, and muttered phrases about "stupid rules." A sense of determination and grit has emerged. I've proven I can multi-task and listen to two children at the same time.

As my last child packed his bags and headed out the door, I suddenly found myself face-to-face with an unexpected houseguest: me. At first, I wasn't sure what to do with this newfound company. I mean, sure, I vaguely remembered who I used to be before the chaos of parenting took over, but did I still know how to make conversation without resorting to discussing the latest episode of *The Office*? Could I handle the quiet without the roar of a *Lord of the Rings* marathon in the background? What would I do with my time if we didn't go through five loves of homemade bread each week? It turns out my culinary skills were a tad rusty after years of serving up chicken nuggets, pizza, and mac 'n' cheese too.

But as the days stretched into weeks, I started to get the hang of this new gig. It included making good on my promise to cultivate new interests. I started listening to podcasts and then decided to host and produce one. There was more time for writing books. Speaking. Decluttering. Gardening and canning didn't make much sense when cooking for two, but stopping at the farmer's market did. We seeded down the vegetable garden plot with grass and kept only the berries and apples.

A Forever Bond

Gradually, and almost imperceptibly, I found myself feeling more at home than ever before—in the quiet embrace of an empty nest filled with endless possibilities. As gradually as my boys had found their independence, I'd also found mine.

In the gradual letting go of my children, I found the courage to hold on to my dreams. And in doing so, I have come to realize that the greatest gift I can give them is not just a place to forever call home but the example of a life well-lived—a life in which I am unapologetically, authentically, and wholeheartedly myself.

And in the spaces they once occupied, I have found not emptiness but joy—the joy of witnessing their growth, their achievements, and the remarkable individuals they have become. Every milestone they reach and every goal they pursue is a testament to their resilience and determination, filling my heart with an indescribable sense of gratitude.

Staying Close When They're Far Away

SUZY MIGHELL

WELL, IT FINALLY HAPPENED. ALL our adult kids moved away. Like, not just out of the house, but away, away. Like, out of town! Like so many other empty nesters, Bob and I were confronted with the issue of how to stay close to our adult kids when we wouldn't get to see them face-to-face regularly.[9]

I heard a relationship expert once say that love is more intensely felt, top-down rather than the other way around. While he didn't mean that we love our kids more than they love us, he did mean that parents will think about their kids more than the other way around. It may sound harsh, but I will say we've found it to be true. I would say it's also true of the other empty-nester couples we know.

This means that, as parents of adult kids, we need to temper our expectations. Expectations are the enemy of contentedness and joy, and they are self-centered rather than others-centered. True love is others-focused (1 Corinthians 13), and that's the kind of love I want to have and the kind of parent of adult kids I want to be.

Suppose you go into interactions with your kids with too many expectations about how things will be. In that case, you're going to be disappointed. My best advice? We all need significance and purpose, but we can't place that expectation on another person. It's just not fair to them. Instead, look for your purpose in your faith, in meaningful work, and in serving others.

Raising kids is a sacred calling, and your kids will always be your kids. That said, I know you know your relationship with them changes as they get older. You shift from instruction and advice-giver to encourager, cheerleader, and (if asked) trusted counselor. If you don't make that shift, you may lose your kids and sacrifice the relationship you want to have with them as adults.

> All relationships need space to breathe, and yet they also require intentionality to grow.

All relationships need space to breathe, and yet they also require intentionality to grow. So, how can you stay close to your adult kids when you don't get to see them face-to-face as often as you'd like? I've discovered five meaningful things that we can do to keep those relationships thriving.

Digital Communication

We're so blessed to live in a time when our kids are just a text, a FaceTime, or a phone call away! Take the time to send funny articles, quotes, or memes to your kids, and react appropriately when they send you one back. My daughter sent me a Reel of a girl who has to call her mom before doing anything, which was, of course, a hilarious exaggeration of our relationship. That's what made it funny!

Remember that digital communication doesn't just go one way. You don't want to be a digital helicopter parent, but at the same time, you don't want to always wait for them to call or text you first. One basic rule of communication to remember is that silence is rarely interpreted positively. If you're constantly waiting for them to make the first move with communication, they may think you don't really care. (Which, of course, couldn't be further from the truth.)

If you miss them, tell them! Ask for a convenient time for a catch-up FaceTime or call. Don't go in with an agenda or expectations. Instead, just enjoy the sweetness of the time together. Spend that time wisely.

Ask them to tell you about work or school.

Ask them to walk you through a typical day in their life.

If they share something tender, painful, or even celebratory, say, "Thank you for sharing that with me." Remember to reflect their feelings in your response. (Romans 12:15: "Be happy with those who are happy, and weep with those who weep.")

If they're ill, hurting, or especially needy, continue to check up on them via text or call in the coming days.

End the conversation well. I always ask my kids what they have coming up that week and how I can pray for them.

Tell them you love them as you sign off!

Get on Their Turf

No matter how old they are, your kids still want you to be proud of them. When you get on their turf, you'll learn so much about them! Showing you where they work, go to school, or even grocery shop is important to them. And seeing it all will give you great insight into their lives and offer the opportunity for some really special conversations. If you're looking for ways to bless and encourage them, getting on their turf will do it!

Help When You Can

When your kids need help, GO! Whether they need help moving, recovering from mononucleosis, getting over a bad breakup, or adjusting to a new baby, go! No matter how old your kids are, trust me, they want their mom when they don't feel well or need help.

When I was down with a sprained ankle for a few days, I was texting my eighty-something-year-old mom daily photos of my discolored foot.

> No matter how old your kids are ... they want their mom when they don't feel well.

Love Who They Love

This extends to their spouses, kids, and even their friends!

When my sons got married, I got two new daughters. My sons love these girls, so I love them too. I work on building my relationships with them, putting them into the same category as my own daughter in my heart. This extends to the practical too. When it comes to gifts, I spend the same amount on each of my kids—including my precious daughters-in-law. When it comes to prayer, I pray for them just like I pray for my own kids.

The young women my sons have married are different from me—and that's a good thing! I don't focus on our differences—I focus on our similarities, and the biggest one of all is they love my sons. I told both girls that I did the best I could with my boys, but I was not the perfect mom, and they were definitely works in progress.

If you struggle with your relationship with your daughter(s)-in-law, or son(s)-in-law, do your best to take your eyes off yourself and focus on what you have in common—love for your son (or daughter). Be very careful not to let your personal expectations (There's that word again!) color your relationship with them. Take your eyes off yourself, pray for them, and ask the Lord to show you how you can serve and bless them.

> Ask the Lord to show you how you can serve and bless them.

Grandparenting is such a joy, and this LouLou cannot get enough! But your adult kids don't stop being your kids when they become parents. In fact, they may need your support and encouragement even more! When our son and his wife were expecting, Bob and I told them that even though we were so excited to be grandparents, the two of them would always be our top priority.

Now, when this sweet family of three walks in the door, we kiss the baby, hug both parents, and always ask how they're doing within the first minute or two. Don't skip over your relationship with your own kids when they have your grandkids! Expand your heart, and take in everyone.

One of our favorite things about becoming grandparents has been seeing our son and daughter-in-law grow into their role as parents. We tell them all the time what an amazing job they're doing, and we do whatever we can to support and encourage them. (The baby snuggles are just an added bonus!)

In addition to their spouses and kids, friends matter. Have you heard millennials called the "friends as family" generation?[10] The first millennials (born in 1981) had just reached their teenage years when *Friends* landed on television screens in 1994. During the highest divorce rates in history, the show about a group of friends who meet up every day to laugh and cry their way through life together became somewhat of a template for our kids' lives. The prevalence of social media only added to this mindset that has come to characterize their generation.

The bottom line is that your adult kids' friends are *very* important to them. Learn their friend's names, remember the things your kids tell you about them, and ask about their friends when you get together.

> Learn their friend's names ... and ask about their friends when you get together.

Show Practical Thoughtfulness

Everyone loves gifts because of what they represent: thoughtfulness. Gift your kids with thoughtfulness as often as you can. It doesn't have to be expensive! Gifts can be experiences, time together, or actual gifts.

When I didn't know what to get my daughter-in-law for her birthday, I called my son. He told me she'd been stressed at work and suggested a spa day. I was able to go online and find the spa he suggested, and by the end of the day, she had a gift certificate in her inbox. Sometimes, providing an experience for your adult child (even if it doesn't involve you) is the most thoughtful thing you can do for them.

When your kids live out of town, spending time together can require some advance planning, but it's worth it.

Another time, when I asked my daughter-in-law what she wanted for her birthday, she told me that she wanted me to take her shopping. She and I spent the sweetest afternoon shopping, then going to our favorite gluten-free/vegan bakery for cupcakes. It was such a fun afternoon together, and we had a great conversation.

There are so many great gift ideas that can help you stay close to your adult kids who live far away. Send a gift of soup when they're sick, of cookies when they're studying, and flowers when you want them to know they're in your thoughts!

Online sources don't only ship flowers. You can also send popcorn, fruit, snack variety boxes, and pop-up cards. Something like a takeout or meal delivery gift card can help relieve the pressure of making dinner when things get busy or stressful.

STAYING CLOSE TO ADULT KIDS who don't live close by takes thoughtfulness and effort, but it makes such a difference. When all else fails, ask them, "How can I help?" Be prepared to act on their answer. Remember to temper your expectations and focus on loving them well by serving them. (Philippians 2:3–4).

It All Adds Up

ROBIN GRUNDER

MY HUSBAND AND I HAVE a blended family of seven children. We used to joke about that number adding up to a lot of laundry, sports uniforms to keep track of, and meals every day. As it turned out, it really wasn't a joke.

But I loved it. Let me clarify. I loved the amount of people we called ours, not the amount of laundry. When Brian and I first got together, our kids' ages and stages ranged from senior in high school down to second grade. I loved being mom to my own. I loved being a bonus mom to Brian's kids.

Needless to say, our calendar was always full. We used a different color to identify each child when jotting our to-dos down. Even if each of our kids were only involved in one extracurricular activity outside the home, the calendar was a rainbow of commitments just about every day.

I specifically remember one evening in the middle of raising our family when we had no place we had to be. No sporting events, no drop-offs to youth groups or practices. I don't know what happened or how it happened, but there we were in a quiet house, in our recliners, and flipping through the channels, finally settling on *Wheel of Fortune*.

Empty Schedule

Two thoughts came to mind. The first—*What am I forgetting?* I figured I had to be forgetting something that I needed to do or someplace I needed to be. The second was, *Do empty nesters watch* Wheel of Fortune? *Because I think I am down for that.*

This no-pressure, no-place-to-be evening was an isolated incident for sure.

I cooked for our party of nine. Three of those nine were hungry football players, and one was their coach. And if we got lucky and all nine were home at the same time for the same meal (a rarity), the odds were good that a few of their friends would be there too. I received many texts that were to the effect of "Mom, what's for supper?"

My response would sometimes reduce the amount I needed to make. I prepared meals as if everyone would be home to eat, but as they grew more independent, I also had to assume that a few would not.

> Gradually, the loads of laundry shrank, and the college tuitions grew.

Gradually, the loads of laundry shrank, and the college tuitions grew. Each time one of our children graduated from high school and moved on to college, the dynamics in our home shifted just a bit. Even though we were still busy, everyone could tell that someone was missing. We would settle into a new collective flow, and a year or two later, another birdie flew the nest.

I'd like to say I handled it all well. But I didn't.

I grieved each time one of our kids moved out. I mourned over all the things we would not do anymore. I mourned over all the things I wish I would have done.

Full Heart

After launching six kids out into the world, almost one right after the other, our youngest daughter was the only one left living at home. Her next oldest sister had just graduated the year before, and she was getting ready for her own graduation from high school in just a couple of months.

It was the class of 2020.

I'm sure I don't have to say much more than that for everyone to know that suddenly, we were no longer going to multiple gymnasiums, school plays, or other events every week. We weren't going to any events. Classes were canceled. Prom was cancelled. Graduation ceremony, postponed. Without warning, life as we knew it was canceled.

My daughter was frustrated, and rightfully so. She didn't get to experience all the "lasts" that she grew up watching her siblings do. It was like someone taking the scissors and cutting her senior year of high school off before reaching the end.

But I have to admit I enjoyed slowing down. I enjoyed our time at home. My youngest daughter got to be "the only child" for a short time. Our conversations weren't just by text. Even our adult children who were sheltering at home in their own corners of the country had a new heart to reconnect. There were a couple of times when my kids all gathered around the living room via a video call, and we played a game that they found that could be done with our phones while live on our video call.

I had my kids "home" on my TV screen. It had been a really long time since all of our schedules allowed for gathering, games, and conversation. It really warms my heart when I think about how much fun I have with my adult children. Of course, I love them. But I like them too.

Multiplied Blessings

Finally, that fall, the last of my babies packed up her little pick-up truck, backed out of our driveway, and drove off to the next chapter of her life.

As the last page of this chapter of motherhood turned, I was left wondering—*What's my next chapter?*

It's not like this was a surprise or we didn't have time to think about it. Or that we hadn't experienced what it was like to have our kids grow up, drive cars, graduate high school, and move away. This was our seventh time. In many ways, my husband and I were looking forward to this chapter. As a blended family, we never actually got to know one another without kids being in the picture. This would be our season.

I've experienced the new rhythms of when each child entered my world—the excitement, the overwhelm, and settling into our new patterns.

And now I've experienced all that comes with each child leaving home—the excitement for their future, the overwhelm and sadness, and again settling into our family's new rhythm. Until finally, after twenty-five years of parenting children at home (or was it just a breath?), the nest was empty.

> One thing cannot be argued—we loved our kids well.

Andy Stanley said, "Your greatest contribution to the kingdom of God may not be something you do but someone you raised."[11] It's true. We weren't perfect parents, and if I'm being honest, there are a lot of things we didn't do right on the parenting front. But one thing cannot be argued—we loved our kids well. We are proud of the grown human beings they have become. It all adds up.

My husband and I are no longer driving in the fast lane. It was a little awkward at first, trying to figure out the dance steps to our new normal. But dance we did as, once again, we have settled into what our lives currently are—an empty-nest life. A physically and mentally slower life with time for lingering and reflection.

And occasionally, *Wheel of Fortune.*

Here's what we're learning after raising a large, blended family—yes, we joked about all the laundry, all the college tuition, and everything "extra" that would add up on a regular basis. But you know what else adds up?

The grandkids.

For us, the next chapter looks pretty *grand!*

It Wasn't Supposed to Be Like This

KIM WILBANKS

HAD A PLAN. IT WAS an excellent one. Like most girls growing up in the 1960s and 1970s, I had my life all figured out exactly how it was supposed to be. You know, go to college, get married, have some kids, live in the same town as those kids, their spouses, and my bevy of grandchildren.

We would spend all the birthdays and holidays together, just like I had done with my parents, grandparents, aunts, uncles, and cousins. I would go shopping with my mother, daughter, and grand-daughter on Saturdays, just like in my childhood. We would go to church together on Sundays, a pew filled with grandchildren, and then come home to Sunday lunch, just like my childhood.

It was going to be great, but something happened along the way. The empty nest was nothing like I had envisioned.

In the Beginning

Following the hiccup of a broken engagement during my senior year of college, I returned home and began looking for my first proper job.

I really wanted to be a wife and mom, and that breakup was my first clue that things do not always go as planned. I had a teaching degree, so I sought a job teaching United States history.

That summer after graduation, I started dating the man who is now my husband. We grew up in the same church, but he was a few years older than me. My grandparents and his parents were good friends, the kind who ate dinner together weekly and sometimes vacationed together. I was aware of him but, because of our age difference, did not know him well.

After some serious, successful matchmaking between our respective relatives, we ended up together and married a little less than two years after our first date. Life was good. We even built a house with a white picket fence.

A couple of years into our marriage, we decided it was time for children, especially since my husband was already in his thirties. (We thought we were so old back then). Imagine my surprise when my first pregnancy ended with a miscarriage. That was certainly not in the plan. I wondered if the stress of teaching middle school contributed to my miscarriage, so I ended my short-lived teaching career.

After five years of marriage, we finally welcomed our firstborn, a son. A little over two years later, his little sister arrived. Our family was complete, or so all the ladies at our church told us. We sold the Hallmark store we owned and moved into the same neighborhood as my parents and my grandmother.

When My Nest Was Full

The growing-up years were memorable. We did all the things—soccer, tap-dancing lessons, ballet lessons, Cub Scouts, horseback riding, band concerts, choir concerts, piano lessons, and church. I became a stay-at-home mom and substitute teacher at the school my kids attended. I volunteered in their classrooms and chaperoned every field trip, except the year my daughter's seventh-grade class toured the water waste management facility. Somehow, I was busy that day.

I hosted birthday parties and took them to their friend's birthday parties. It was not uncommon to have friends over for slumber parties or Sunday play dates after church. We went on family trips to the beach, the mountains, all over the United States, and even overseas. When they were in their teens, we even went on a few mission trips together. We were busy, busy, busy.

> Reality set in when my son was in the tenth grade.

Reality set in when my son was in the tenth grade. I remember walking down the street in my neighborhood one evening, tears streaming down my face, thinking to myself, *This is all about to end.* It was time to look at colleges, beef up GPAs, and stress over SAT scores. Not to mention, both of my teens were now expressing their independence, as they should. I wasn't ready for them to grow up.

We had a hectic junior and senior year of high school, followed by another hectic junior and senior year of high school. And somehow, in all our college visits, my two Florida kids chose Alabama colleges. They were both gone so fast, like the three little pigs who set out to seek their fortunes in a far-off land. It didn't bother me at first, not really. Okay, maybe it did. But they chose excellent schools that were smack dab in the middle of the Bible belt. Besides that, they were fun to visit.

For two of the years, my son and daughter were an hour apart from each other, so there were many fun road trips to Alabama. We got to know all the routes and all the best restaurants.

Leaving the Nest

Unfortunately, neither child got the memo that they were supposed to come home after graduation. My daughter stayed put in

Birmingham, her college town, where she married one of her classmates. My son went on to graduate school in Nashville, where he remains to this day. He married a third-generation local girl. They are the parents of my delightful little grandson, and another will join the family soon. It has been over a decade since their graduations, so I am pretty sure they are not coming home as *I* had planned. Sigh.

> Neither child got the memo that they were supposed to come home after graduation.

My children didn't follow my plan to have them find a spouse close to home and provide me with lots of grandchildren who would live close by. But thank goodness they didn't because they both married well. We love our son-in-law and daughter-in-law. I call the four of them my peeps.

It's difficult living so far from my children, especially now since there are grandchildren. I see them most holidays, but it's the day-to-day that I really miss. I would love to pop by to see my grandson, meet my daughter for coffee or have everyone over for dinner—the normal things families do together. I love my children and enjoy spending time with them.

You might wonder why I don't just pick up and move closer. It seems like the reasonable thing to do. My husband and I have discussed it often. But it isn't as simple as it seems. We like where we live; it's mild in the winter, and we rarely have tornados like Alabama and Tennessee. Our doctors and friends are here, and being in our sixties, there are a lot of doctors. We are a short drive to one of our favorite places, an island beach on the Gulf of Mexico.

For the past two years, we have been occupied with settling the estates of both my parents, who passed away, which is another aspect of the empty nest I didn't expect so soon. It is a lot. Also, our children love to travel, and who is to say they won't pick up and move elsewhere? Right now, it's easy for us to visit them often, so I sense the call to wait.

Lessons Learned

I have learned two important things in my life, particularly in these empty-nest years. First, life is rarely what you think it will be, but that is not necessarily a bad thing. There are so many things in my life that are not at all what I expected, yet I have had a good life. I have done so many things and traveled to so many places I never would have imagined.

Second, and more importantly, waiting on God and trusting his plan for my life rather than my own makes me more content. I'm learning to look expectantly for what he has in store for me, even if it isn't according to my plan. That's a big part of the adventure of living in the empty nest.

Learning to Open Jars by Myself

MEL TAVARES

HID MY TEARS BEHIND A smile and waved as he backed the U-Haul and trailered car out of our driveway and headed to Kansas. Once he rounded the corner out of sight, I stopped waving and made my way back into the house, sobbing uncontrollably. My nest was empty.

Letting go starts the day our babies are born, but it is not an easy process. Because of gaps in births, I'd been actively parenting over three decades. It wasn't easy when any of them left, but this time was the worst. He was my baby, the only boy, and had been solo in the nest for the past decade. I spent days wandering in and out of his bedroom, walking down memory lane as I looked at trophies and souvenirs he'd left for me to "hold on to" for him.

Memorabilia Galore

Decade's worth of memories filled the gaping wound of loneliness with smiles and joy. The Boy Scout memorabilia filled an entire shelf, including Pinewood Derby cars, *Scout Life* magazines, and troop pictures. I thought back to the years of ironing his uniform, sewing on badges, driving him to meetings, ensuring he had the camping gear needed, driving him to Scout camp for weeks in the summer, and the joy of seeing him move up through the ranks to achieve Eagle Scout. Memories of our lawn becoming a place for his Scout friends to gather for "Grill and Chill" weekends flashed through my mind, and I caught myself laughing out loud as I recalled some of their antics.

Another shelf held football, soccer, and basketball trophies and photos. The years spent on the sidelines flashed before me as I recalled the thrill of victory and agony of defeat and the meals we inevitably consumed after the games. I recalled the New England championship soccer game played in the snow with the wind biting through the layers of clothing. Still transported back in time, I heard my own voice cheering him on, "Go, Myles!"

Jolted back to the present, I glanced at the wall and smiled as I remembered standing with him in the rain to get the autographed picture of our hometown hero, NASCAR driver Joey Logano. Next to it was a burst hot water bottle, autographed by the Xtreme Impact team that had visited and demonstrated feats of strength. I looked at the bulletin board filled with concert and movie ticket stubs. Pinned in the corner was a letter from the college he'd attended 1300 miles from home. While there, he met his now-wife, and because of their love, he chose to move to the Midwest.

> The reality started to sink in, and I realized I needed to shift my mindset to the future.

I cried as I spoke aloud in the empty room. "He's moved to the Midwest. He didn't leave for a camping weekend with the Scouts, or for another mission trip, or to attend another semester of college. This time, it's a permanent move." The reality started to sink in, and I realized I needed to shift my mindset to the future, just as he had.

Flashbacks in Time

My role in life has been redefined and expanded. As a wife, I am able to give more time and attention to my husband. We've started taking more day trips and weekend trips. I developed new routines, new menus, and grocery lists and heeded the words of my son, who told me, "You will need to learn to open jars by yourself." (I bought a jar opener.)

Dinner is served later because we aren't working around school and sports schedules. Meals are smaller and take less time to cook. There is no longer a need to schedule showers or use laundry machines. Evenings are relaxed, and bedtime is no longer determined by waiting until the kids have safely returned to the nest for the night.

Coping with the emotions that come with an empty nest and letting go doesn't mean there aren't still times of nostalgia. Living in the city means our son isn't the only one who enjoys loud exhausts. Every time a young man steps down on the gas going past our house, I long to hear my son pull into the driveway at midnight just one more time. Passing old classic trucks on the road still flashes me back to days of him working on his truck with his buddies, who offered moral support while eating my homemade cookies. I cannot see a Boy Scout or watch sports events without feeling a twinge, wishing for the clocks to turn back one more time.

As the weeks turned to months, I discovered some blessings of being an empty nester. Like many empty nesters, I'd placed my own wants, needs, and desires on the backburner during the active parenting years. I'd not spent much time thinking about these things for over thirty years. Missing the day-to-day routine is a challenge, but I have learned to prioritize my mental well-being.

Reinventing

I'm learning to reimagine and reinvent myself as I navigate life as an empty nester. I take time to sit in the quiet and drink my morning coffee, something I dreamed of doing as a mother of very active children. Showers are no longer limited to a quick in and out, and there's even time for a nice leisurely soak in the old claw foot tub. I play music that I like when at home or in the car, which often includes "old school" praise music or classic rock, neither of which are always appreciated by the younger generations.

When I reach into the candy bowl for a piece of my favorite chocolate, I know there is some left because there are no kids home to eat it. Reading a book has become a favorite way to spend an afternoon in the reading nook I created in a reimagined bedroom turned podcast studio. Serving in the local church and community has been a core value of our family life, and although activities have changed, my commitment to others in need remains a vital part of maintaining my mental well-being.

> I miss the day-to-day, ordinary things that having a full nest brings.

The age gap between my kids resulted in having several grandkids prior to our youngest leaving the nest. Although no longer responsible for decorating birthday cakes or creating leprechaun shenanigans or hiding Easter eggs, I am grateful we are included in many of the festivities as our adult children carry on traditions with their own children.

My daughters sometimes get tired of coordinating special occasions, just like I used to, and seem surprised when I say how much I miss creating all the memories. Not only do I miss special celebrations, but I also miss the day-to-day, ordinary things that having a full nest brings. Like baking.

Baking and Boxing

Baking is my love language. My postmaster knows who the package is for every time I walk in with my arms full. He smiles and asks, "Is that for your son?" I always nod and say, "Fragile and perishable," knowing there is little need to articulate after all the years of sending home-baked cookies, cakes, and candies to the Midwest. He understands having children leave and move long distances, as several of his own have flown the nest and moved hundreds of miles away. We reminisce a bit and then say our goodbyes until it is time for the next box of love to be sent out.

The number of hours a day mothers spend cooking, cleaning, doing laundry, and driving kids to and from activities is incredible. Having an empty nest means extra hours in the day and week. One of my favorite things to do is to meet friends for coffee, and I make it a point to meet someone at least once a week, free from the need to keep an eye on the clock and go to the school. Indeed, a significant benefit is being able to talk or video chat without constant interruptions during the call. Having freedom in the schedule to accept a last-minute invitation is still a foreign concept, but one I am adjusting to.

> He only loaned them to me for a short while to train them up for him and then let them fly.

I've known from the beginning that children are a gift from God, and he only loaned them to me for a short while to train them up for him and then let them fly for the purposes he has created them for. I diligently sacrificed and did all I knew to do to raise each child to be productive adults, capable of handling whatever life throws at them, equipped to succeed in their chosen occupations, and able to raise families of their own.

Pride causes my heart to swell as I reflect on who they have become and all they are doing with their lives, and as I continue to learn to live as an empty nester, I rejoice in watching them grow and flourish. Thankfully, there is still an opportunity to influence them, and they call for counsel and guidance during this new season in our lives.

I remain grateful for the years my nest was full and for the times when they return with their families and the nest fills up again, if only for a weekend. And then, I'll surely ask someone to open a jar for me—for old time's sake.

God's Unexpected Provision

PAM WHITLEY TAYLOR

OUR DAUGHTER HAD NEVER HAD any overnight slumber parties. She'd never spent a night at Grandma's without me, never attended a girlfriend's birthday party, and never been on any school trips as her brother had. There had been no opportunities for me to gradually let go. Overnight, in a heartbeat, her room was left empty, and so was our nest. This mama's heart was shattered.

The Beginning of Nesting Instincts

I'd just completed my sophomore quarter of college at Southern Miss as my fiancé graduated from his university in Oklahoma. I dropped out of USM, and we married over the Christmas holidays.

As a baby boomer, my greatest dream had always been to meet my Prince Charming, become a wife, and then a mom. Perhaps I'd heard the story of Cinderella a few too many times. My new husband and I settled happily into married life, and by the time I was twenty-two, our first baby was born, an adorable baby boy. I loved being a wife, and I adored becoming a mom.

Four and a half years later, our second child was born. We were delighted when baby number two was a dark-haired little girl. We named her Jan. She also happened to be Oklahoma City's first baby of the year, born January 1 at 12:54 a.m. We were on channel 4 and channel 5 by the time she was only a few hours old. Our family seemed perfect—we had a boy and now a girl.

> Our family seemed perfect—we had a boy and now a girl.

A Tender Fledgling

Jan was eight days old when she turned purple, and we rushed frantically to the nearest ER. After many tests, we were told our sweet baby was born with a heart defect that was undetectable at birth. Open-heart surgery ensued. During that rushed intervention, Jan went into shock and stopped breathing for fifteen minutes. They were able to revive her. However, those oxygen-deprived moments caused major havoc to her brain.

I was twenty-seven years old and had no medical training when I became Jan's caregiver. That was long before Google existed, and I learned through trial and error how to handle her major health issues.

Many people heard of our plight by word of mouth and rallied to help us. The most wonderful help came from an ER nurse whose name I never knew. She heard of our struggle to feed Jan and sent us several three-ounce syringes, and I learned to feed Jan drop by drop.

As I was thrust onto that lonely road called caregiving, in his grace, God armed me with Psalm 139:13. "You made all the delicate, inner parts of my body and knit me together in my mother's womb." I knew that applied to me as well as to Jan. I also learned that God was the only one who would be with me and Jan through every one of those years of long, dark, seizure-riddled nights.

Soaring Along

Life flew by as we jumped from one crisis to another. In addition to a very weak sucking reflex, we discovered that Jan had a damaged thermostat, very little vision, and a seizure disorder. On top of that, we were told she'd probably not live to be three. Other specialists told us Jan would never walk, talk, or use her hands. One even told us she'd never smile or respond in any way. Her prognosis was extremely grim.

Over the years, as we and hundreds prayed, our sweet girl developed far beyond all those hopeless predictions. No, she never did learn to walk or talk or use her hands, but she learned to love and adore life. She squealed with delight at the silliest things and laughed with abandon at repeated words such as sassafras, sassafras tea, or Susan, Susan, Susan.

She also adored certain sounds. If a person could mimic Donald Duck's shrill voice, they could entertain her and themselves until they both ran out of breath. And Jan developed an amazing love for music. She was very opinionated about what she liked though. If we played her favorites, she was as happy as a bear in a beehive.

> She taught us and others so many amazing life lessons.

She taught us and others so many amazing life lessons even though she remained forever our baby, except for her size. And against all medical predictions, Jan ultimately lived to be twenty-eight years old. I never thought much about the future because I thought, perhaps, our nest would never be empty.

Those years careened by, and by the time I was in my early forties, Jan's weight and size had increased significantly. My five-foot-two frame remained the same, and it became progressively more difficult to lift Jan. One day, the realization hit me that I was going to lose my health if I continued to push my body day after day. Those long nights of walking her when she cried like a colicky baby were becoming next to impossible to handle. I was totally spent. Finally, I cried out to God.

Hatching a Plan

Within weeks of my prayer, an unexpected door opened for our sweet girl to enter a nearby pediatric nursing center—one of only seven in the United States, one that was only five miles from our front door. I'd never expected to walk through such a door, but with Jan's weight nearing eighty pounds as her seventeenth birthday approached, it became a necessary step—a step I'd never expected to take.

> When I realized that God's plan might be different from what I'd imagined, I was rather shocked.

I'd never considered that Jan's care would ever exceed my abilities because of all the dire predictions from her medical team over the years. But when I realized that God's plan might be different from what I'd imagined, I was rather shocked. How could I possibly turn her care over to strangers? It soon became apparent that I had no choice.

Our son was already a junior in college when the placement date arrived. For three weeks prior, I'd labeled each sock, hair bow, and music CD that Jan owned, along with every piece of clothing. And then, in the blink of an eye, overnight, our nest was empty.

There had been no opportunities to gradually let go—just suddenly overnight an empty lap and an empty room. My mother's heart was not prepared, and I entered a dark tunnel of grief. The hardest part was that I didn't recognize I was grieving because I thought grief occurred only with a death.

I couldn't sleep and would call the pediatric center off and on throughout the night to see how Jan was doing. Often, I'd hear her music playing in the background. I spent much of my days running back and forth to see her. For a season, Jan's health seemed to worsen, and that further added to my grief. I felt I'd failed Jan and God.

I'd burst into tears when I walked back into the silence of our home. It had been filled with Jan's music and her laughter for years. Out of habit, I constantly checked my watch to see if it was time to feed or change her.

I found it difficult to be at home, which felt like an empty tomb. I'd find excuses to not be there until I knew my hubby was close to home. Finally, I started to work part time at our church, and that helped me emotionally. I also learned that leaving music playing in our home helped with the "too quiet" problem when I did come home.

Thankfully, as the months passed, Jan's health gradually improved, and I saw clearly that a fresh set of caregivers every eight hours, 24/7, could do a much better job than one tired mama.

Only then did I recognize God's mighty provision in Jan's placement—not only was it a provision for her, but for me and my whole family. Beautiful doors opened. I could now visit my son at college and take him to lunch, and I could also accompany my husband on his out-of-town travel days. The change I had not wanted turned out to be a wonderful blessing.

Migrating to a New Roost

A few years after Jan's placement, we moved to a new home to be nearer our son and his sweet wife. They were expecting our first grandchild, and we were beyond excited. But that move brought an unexpected ambush of that old empty-nest grief.

We'd not moved in twenty years, and as I packed, I sorted all our worldly goods. As we arrived at our new home with our years of collected belongings in tow, I referred to two of the bedrooms as Ben's and Jan's and kept saying to the movers, "That goes in Ben's room," pointing to the room I'd designated as his, or "That goes in Jan's room!"

What am I doing? I thought. *Jan nor Ben will never live under our roof again.*

> I gradually I embraced our new season and learned to love it.

It took me a day or two to identify that the old empty-nest syndrome had struck my heart one last time. I grieved for a few days and finally decided to order a book written by another empty nester. It was very helpful and aided me in understanding my varied emotions.

With thanksgiving, I gradually embraced our new season and learned to love it. I learned to apply the words of Psalm 118:24, which says, "This is the day the LORD has made. We will rejoice and be glad in it."

Redefining the OC

MICHELLE RAYBURN

A S OUR SECOND CHILD PACKED up and headed to college, Phil and I found ourselves in that awkward limbo between parenthood and retirement. It's a pretty big gap for many of us, and as we get those quarterly retirement fund statements, the gap between launching kids and retirement keeps widening.

We might be working until we're centenarians. I mistakenly wrote centurion at first, which would be much funnier than being one hundred years old. Neither of us planned to command an army. But we did realize we needed to take command of our future.

We were back to the OC, the Original Couple who married in 1989 as baby-faced, clueless young adults. We got a few clues, took on the titles of mom and dad, and forged ahead, basically making up the plan as we went. Now, here we were with a slight bit of gray at our temples but with a lot of life left in these old bones. What next?

Considering Our New Reality

The church we were attending at the time had a small group for older adults called Some Income, No Kids. SINKS for short. It covered the range from around age forty-five to numbers where we prefer to stop counting.

I couldn't bring myself to join. "It's for old people," I said. Just the name SINKS conjured up undesirable images—SINKing feelings. Let me press pause for a moment. Nothing I'm about to say is with any judgment toward older people or empty nesters. It's going to sound that way. Welcome to my identity crisis, which I will title "Becoming That Which I Said I Never Would and Eating Crow."

When you're on the youngish side for becoming empty nesters yet too old to crash the frat party down the street, it warps your thinking a bit. After spending two decades as a mostly stay-at-home mom, I wasn't exactly ready to take up bingo, knit curtains, or get "remotely" close—yes, puns are my love language—to the stage where I needed to cover all of the buttons on the remote with tape so I knew which two to press. Nope.

> It sounded like voluntarily signing up to complain about aches and pains, discuss arthritis and diabetes medications, and swap info about early bird specials.

SINKS sounded in my rebellious mind like voluntarily signing up to complain about aches and pains, discuss arthritis and diabetes medications, and swap info about early bird specials. That all sounded much too close to Wilford Brimley and his long commercials for "dia-be-tis" and Medicare. If you're too young to know who Wilford Brimley is, just use "the Google."

Instead, I started a new career in marketing and social media with a crew of people younger than me, some of them younger than my children.

Creating Adventure

It had been a hot minute since I dusted off my resume. There wasn't much on it, actually, but thanks to a decade or so of attending writer's conferences and dabbling in the writing world while raising our sons, I had a few skills. And I'd completed a Master of Arts in ministry leadership online between parental duties and late-night study sessions. Besides, we needed a second paycheck. My little side gig of teaching piano lessons was no longer covering our healthcare costs. Have you noticed how expensive income taxes are when you have no dependents to deduct?

> Have you noticed how expensive income taxes are when you have no dependents to deduct?

Through some connections I'd made as a writer, I found a job at a marketing agency that also ran a regional magazine. The previous daily uniform of casual jersey knit clothing morphed into business attire, a convenient excuse to go shopping for a new wardrobe, including shoes with heels.

New activities became part of my regular routine: getting my nails done at a salon, commuting to work, meetings with CEOs and clients, and stops on the way home to "pick up something quick" for supper. Along with this came something stay-at-home moms don't have: paid vacation days, bi-weekly paychecks for having conversations with adults, and company lunches and recreational activities.

This all led to some adaptation on the part of the OC. We would often find our own easy meals, eating supper at the times when it worked best for us. Me when I arrived home from my commute ravenous and ready to inhale every snack in arm's reach. And Phil when he came in from puttering in the garage and in the mood for pizza. Never in a million years would I have imagined this casual arrangement after home cooking, canning, and bread baking forever.

Our different waking times, combined with our mutual snoring decibels, preferences for vastly different temperatures, and the availability of now-vacant rooms led us to decide to claim our own sleeping spaces. Before you write letters to me: we love each other, and no one is here to know if we sneak across the hall for visits. *Wink.*

Communicating Our Desires

This redefining has adapted over the last decade. I traded the marketing job for working from home as my own boss—goodbye, commute. And we realized that we still need to be intentional about our relationship. We had to communicate about some of the gritty stuff we'd swept under the rug in the years when we thought ignoring conflict would make it go away. We wrote about that in our book *Classic Marriage: Staying in Love as Your Odometer Climbs.* Without the distractions of kids' activities and church commitments, we came face-to-face with each other and the reality that our communication needed an overhaul.

> We realized that we still need to be intentional about our relationship.

We've discussed our dreams and fulfilled some of them. In the mid-eighties, a high-school-aged Phil had noticed a new resort along Lake Superior on one of his trips up north to the Minnesota Boundary Waters Canoe Area. Somewhere in the back of his mind, he filed away a dream to take his wife there someday. Our funds were always tight in the years when the boys were at home, and we never took a vacation with just the two of us. A weekend here or there, but never more.

Committing to Quality Time

In the year of our twenty-fifth anniversary, both boys were in college, and Phil had his first ministry sabbatical. For the first time ever, we traveled together for more than a few days, visiting family on the West Coast, staying at a friend's cabin up north during peak fall color, and enjoying a timeshare week in Branson gifted by a family member.

Go big or go home was our travel motto after all those years without. We spent three of the seven weeks of his leave on the road.

> We decided to make regular getaways together part of our empty nest life.

This set a new precedent, where we decided to make regular getaways together part of our empty nest life. The following year, I had my first paid vacation at the new job, and we scheduled a stay at the resort he'd been dreaming of for three decades. It has become our new favorite.

It took us all those years to discover how much we both enjoy unplugging from life and relaxing in a condo right on the big water of Lake Superior. How much we enjoy exploring scenic overviews, hiking wooded trails to find waterfalls, and cooking meals together instead of eating out.

After successfully launching two humans into the world, we also have more confidence about revisiting difficult conversations. The come-to-Jesus moments don't freak us out. A few years ago, one of those was about how this total independence thing might not be the best for our relationship. The haphazard schedule of new hobbies and shared time with kids and grandkids hadn't left room for the OC. A tough conversation led to deciding to designate one night a week to cook a meal together and hang out—playing a game, going for a hike, or watching a movie—for an at-home date night.

WHETHER IT'S THE OC OR the OM (Original Me for single parents) or the NC (New Couple for the empty nester starting over as a blended family), we know that each family has its own version of the process. How we each consider, create, communicate, and commit will look vastly different.

I realize now that our current rendition of life in our empty nest looks a bit more like SINKS than I'd care to admit. Phil and I sit around and talk about our aching joints. I remind him to order more blood pressure pills and arthritis meds. We help each other figure out why the buttons on the remote won't cooperate. Our hair is grayer. We're both working full-time (some income), and the nest is empty (no kids).

The path I most resisted has become the path of least resistance. And it's actually quite nice.

Final Thoughts

I HOPE YOU HAVE DISCOVERED camaraderie in our stories. We're your people. While each parent's journey is different, we know that change is the universal experience for all of us. It can feel a lot like transitioning from a rocky trail to a swinging rope bridge. Those freak me out, by the way. Our feet falter a little as we're uncertain exactly where to place each one.

That's normal, but none of us needs to do this alone. We need others for support. Lean on your spouse, your friends, and support networks, or reach out to one of us via the websites listed in the Meet the Authors section that follows. We're happy to give you a virtual hug, a listening ear, or an encouraging word. And if you have a friend who could use inspiration, I hope you'll share this book with them.

If you're feeling the pressure to find your footing, there's no rush to figure it all out. Trust that your path unfolds just as it should, even if it's vastly different from the experiences depicted in this book. Pause to appreciate the incredible job you've done of raising your children. You've earned a break. Or at least a bowl of ice cream.

Life after kids can be vibrant and full of adventure. Here's to your reimagined empty nest.

NOTES

1   "Flamingo," San Diego Zoo Wildlife Alliance Animals and Plants, accessed May 15, 2024, https://animals.sandiegozoo.org/animals/flamingo.

2   First appeared in: Linda Hanstra, "Hide, Ride, then Hit Your Stride: A 3-Step Approach to Empty Nesting," *Empty-Nest Joyride!* (blog), August 27, 2023, Substack, https://lindahanstra.substack.com/p/hide-ride-then-hit-your-stride-empty-nesting/.

3   Portions of this chapter first appeared at: Michele Morin, "Awkward Questions of the Empty Nest and Answers Shaped by Love," *Living Our Days* (blog), October 18, 2023, https://michelemorin.net/2023/10/18/awkward-questions-empty-nest-answers-love/.

4   Madeleine L'Engle, *A Circle of Quiet* (New York: Farrar, Straus and Giroux, 1972) 199.

5   Gretchen Rubin, *The Happiness Project* (New York: HarperCollins Publishers, 2009), as quoted on GoodReads, accessed May 27, 2024, https://www.goodreads.com/work/quotes/6587328.

6   Michelle Rayburn, "'Don't Touch Me' Barbie," *Life Repurposed with Michelle Rayburn* (Substack blog), May 10, 2024, https://michellerayburn.substack.com/p/dont-touch-me-barbie.

7   This chapter first appeared in: Deb DeArmond, *We May Be Done, But We're Not Finished* (Plymouth, MA: Elk Lake Publishing, 2021) 37.

8   Ted Goodman, editor, *Forbes Book of Quotations: 10,000 Thoughts on the Business of Life* (New York: Running Press, 2016), 262.

9   This first appeared at: Suzy Mighell, "5 Meaningful Ways To Stay Close To Adult Kids Living Far Away," *Empty Nest Blessed* (blog), October 9, 2023, https://empty-nestblessed.com/2023/10/09/stay-close-adult-kids/.

10 Clare Thorp, "Friends: The Show that Changed Our Idea of Family," BBC, September 20, 2019, https://www.bbc.com/culture/article/20190920-friends-the-show-that-changed-our-idea-of-family.

11 Andy Stanley, Twitter (X), post by himself, April 17, 2023, accessed May 31, 2024. https://x.com/AndyStanley/status/324713440541290498?lang=en.

Meet the Authors

BETH BARRON worked cross-culturally for thirty-two years, first in the Middle East and now in the US. She teaches English to refugees and uses her writing skills to advocate for them. Beth enjoys connecting heart-to-heart with other women. She graduated from Rice University in Houston and has studied at Dallas Theological Seminary. Beth has published poetry and non-fiction in publications that include *Fathom Magazine* and *DTS Voice*. She blogs regularly at blogs.bible.org.

KIM CUSIMANO is a wife and mother to four. She writes to encourage special needs families and long-term caregivers. Kim and her husband like to think of themselves as hybrid empty nesters. They have launched two young adults and have two special needs young adults in their home. Parenting young children and navigating the school years are behind them. They are enjoying finding new adventures as a party of four! Visit Kim at www.fulljoyministries.com.

PASTOR JENN DAFOE-TURNER is a speaker, contributing author of *Radical Abundance*, Strengthsfinders coach, and acquisitions editor for Abundance Books. She used to be a victim, a slave to addiction, thinking everyone was out to get her. She blamed everyone for her bad choices. Then she met Jesus, the missing piece. She loves to journey with people to experience freedom in every area of their lives. She speaks wisdom to the struggling heart. www.jenndafoe-turner.com

DEB DEARMOND is a successful author, speaker, mentor, and certified writing coach. With six published books and more than 400 published articles, she's written for several Christian magazines, including *Focus on the Family* and James Dobson. Her monthly column, My Purpose Now, is in its eleventh year and is published by Lifeway's *Mature Living* magazine, which has an international circulation of 300,000 monthly readers.

Speaker, author, podcaster, **SUE DONALDSON** and her husband, Mark, have raised three daughters in San Luis Obispo, CA, who keep them at the bank and on their knees. Sue loves connecting people to one another, to God, and to his Word, and has been speaking for the last twenty years. View eight retreat series, sixteen keynotes, at WelcomeHeart.com. Sue hosts a weekly podcast: *Welcome Heart: Living a Legacy Life* and a free Facebook group: Welcome Heart, Welcome Home. You're invited!

RUTHIE GRAY is a wife, Gigi, empty nester, and content marketing consultant for Christian creatives, specializing in Instagram and newsletter growth. Her hobbies include Florida beach walks, RVing with hubby, and reading historical fiction. Ruthie is the founder of Authentic Online Marketing School, and podcasts at *Authentic Online Marketing* (so easy, your mom— or Carol Brady—can do it). Connect with her on Instagram or her website at authenticonlinemarketing.com.

ROBIN GRUNDER is a journalist, author, ghostwriter, and executive editor of Legacy Press Books. Her work has been featured in *Chicken Soup for the Soul,* regional and national parenting publications, newspapers, and several ghostwritten books. She is the author of *Memoir in the Margins of Psalms: Journaling Your Life-Story in the Margins of God's Story.* Robin and her husband, Brian, have a blended family of seven adult children and three grandchildren. Visit Robin at www.robingrunder.org.

LINDA HANSTRA, a semi-retired speech-language pathologist, writes about what brings joy to her empty nest—faith, family, cycling, traveling, grandparenting, and more—at lindahanstra.com and on Substack. The author of *Lent through the Little Things*, Linda and her husband, Tom, live in southwest Michigan and spend summers "Up North" in Minnesota, their home away from home. With four adult children, one daughter-in-love, and two adorable grandchildren, they are cruising along on their "empty-nest joyride!"

KOLLEEN LUCARIELLO is the author of *#beYOU: Change Your Identity One Letter at a Time*, a writer, speaker, and co-executive director of Activ8Her, Inc., a ministry focused on creating connection in relationship, building confidence in leadership, and developing courageous faith in women. She and her hubby, Pat, have been journeying through life together for forty-plus years. She's mom to three adult married children and Mimi to six fabulous grandchildren. Let's connect at speakkolleen.com.

SUZY MIGHELL is the personality and content creator behind Google's top-ranked empty nester blog and social media brand Empty Nest Blessed. Follow Suzy at EmptyNestBlessed.com or search @emptynestblessed on social media. She shares everything from fashion and beauty, to travel, wellness, parenting, and more! Known for her love of color, enthusiasm, and joyful spirit, she shares her life with her followers while creating content to encourage and inspire them.

MAUREEN MILLER is an award-winning author who writes for her local newspaper, is a contributing writer for *Guideposts*, and a featured blogger for several online devotional websites. She's also contributed to more than twenty collaborative projects to date. She loves life in all its forms and enjoys it with her husband, Bill, and their three children and grandchildren on Selah Farm—their hobby homestead nestled in the mountains of western North Carolina. She blogs at www.penningpansies.com, sharing God's extraordinary character in the ordinary things of life, and she's finishing her first novel, *Gideon's Book*.

KELLY WILSON MIZE is a wife, mother of two young adults, and former educator with a master's degree in education. In twenty-plus years as a published author, she has composed numerous articles, interviews, curriculum projects, and devotions—including contribution to eleven books. Credits include Lifeway, Bethany House, Guideposts, (in)courage, and others. Her first picture book, *The Beautiful Story Within Me*, was published in 2021.

MICHELE MORIN is a Bible teacher, writer, reader, and gardener committed to the truth that women can become confident Christ-followers and students of God's Word. She has been married to an unreasonably patient husband for thirty-plus years, and together they have four married sons and six adorable grandchildren. Active in educational ministries with her local church, Michele delights in sitting at a table surrounded by women with open Bibles.

ROBYN MULDER lives in South Dakota with her husband, Pastor Gary Mulder. Their four children (and two adorable grandchildren) all live in Lincoln, Nebraska (at least for now). Robyn writes about faith, productivity, and mental health at www.robynmulder.com. Having an empty nest gave her a little extra time, and she finally published her first book: *Staying Away from the Edge: Help and Hope for Living after a Mental Health Diagnosis.*

MICHELLE RAYBURN is an author and host of the *Life Repurposed* podcast who helps others find hope in the trashy stuff of life. She has an MA in ministry leadership and writes Christian living books, humor, and Bible studies. Together with her husband, they've raised two sons and gained two daughters-in-law—plus four grandchildren. Dark chocolate, an iced coffee, and a good book in the hammock top Michelle's favorites list. Find her musings on Substack at *Life Repurposed with Michelle Rayburn* or connect at www.michellerayburn.com.

LYNETA SMITH is the author of multiple-award-winning *Curtain Call: A Memoir* and dozens of other articles and stories. She and her husband are happy empty nesters with the tiniest laundry room ever in their downsized townhome in Middle Tennessee. When she's not writing or editing, you can find her chatting with friends at the local coffee shop or volunteering in her local church. Come connect with her at www.LynetaSmith.com.

SHARON SUNKLE is the author of *I Will Mentor You,* a guidebook for mentoring women. She has written a second book, a devotional, soon to be released. Sharon has written several articles for numerous outlets and been speaker at several women's events. She has taught Bible studies and mentored other women for more than twenty-five years. Sharon is married to Richard, has three sons, two daughters-in-law, and eight grandchildren. She lives in Southern California. Reach her at s.sunkle17@yahoo.com.

PAM WHITLEY TAYLOR is a wife, mother, and grandmother. She was a speaker for Christian Women's Club for many years. Both her testimony and writings share the tools she found to fight for hope, contentment, and joy in the midst of heartache and grief. Look for her book *God's Grace Keeps Pace* on Amazon. You can find her stories in several compilations, including Guidepost books. She now lives in Oklahoma with her sweet husband, John, where she enjoys photography and travel.

MEL TAVARES is an empty nester who loves it when her grown and flown children and grandchildren return for a visit. She is an award-winning author, speaker, and certified Christian life coach. Mel loves to encourage and equip women to live in the fullness of their purpose, including when their nest is empty. Empty nesters may find her best-selling book *21 Days to Mental Well-Being* helpful. Her website is drmeltavares.com.

LORI VOBER suffered a hemorrhagic stroke at age twenty-nine and then developed epilepsy from the stroke. She is a survivor, overcomer, and connector who is passionate about sharing hope with others. With the right perspective, attitude, and perseverance, we can stay unstuck and keep moving forward. Even with her difficulties, Lori and her husband, Dainis, were able to become adoptive parents to a sibling group of three. Lori's journey and books can be found at www.lorivober.com.

KIM WILBANKS is a wife and mom with two grown, married children and one grandson. She and her husband of forty years are lifelong residents of Florida who enjoy spending time at the beach and the mountains of North Carolina. Kim enjoys reading, crafting, jigsaw puzzles, travel, history, and her labradoodle, Boone. She is a believer who enjoys Bible studies and mission trips. You can find her writing about empty nest life at www.kimwilbanks.com.

LISA-ANNE WOOLDRIDGE is inspired by illuminated manuscripts and stained-glass windows. Her heartwarming true stories have been published in several popular collections. Her second novel, *The Cozy Cat Bookstore Mysteries—The Rose and Crown*, is now available online. She lives in the land of mountains and valleys that drink in the rain of heaven—otherwise known as Oregon, or you may find her at www.Lisa-Anne.net.

If you enjoyed this Life Repurposed compilation,
check out the others in the series.

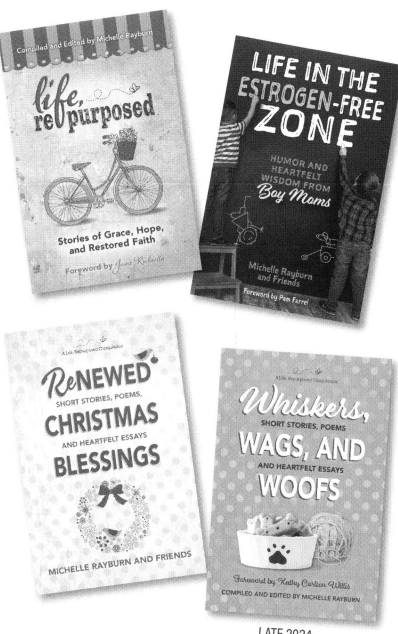

LATE 2024

Made in the USA
Columbia, SC
10 November 2024